# AIR FRYER RECIPES COOKBOOK 2023

## With Pictures

120 Everyday Homemade Meals for
Your Quick and Easy Air Frying

LOUIE PRESTON

**Warning-Disclaimer**

The purpose of this book is to educate and entertain. The author or publisher does not guarantee that anyone following the techniques, suggestions, tips, ideas, or strategies will become successful. The author and publisher shall have neither liability or responsibility to anyone with respect to any loss or damage caused, or alleged to be caused, directly or indirectly by the information contained in this book.

# Table of Contents


Introduction 1

CHAPTER 1: BREAKFAST RECIPES 2

Air Fryer Breakfast Pizza ..... 3
Air Fryer Banana Bread ..... 3
Air Fryer Crispy Breakfast Burritos ..... 4
Air fryer Monkey Bread ..... 4
Air Fryer Breakfast Frittata ..... 5
Air Fryer French Toast ..... 5
Air Fryer Breakfast Potatoes ..... 6
Air Fryer Cinnamon French Toast ..... 6
Air Fryer Fried Simple Eggs ..... 7
Air Fryer Apple Pie Egg Rolls ..... 7
Air Fryer Pancakes ..... 8
Air Fryer Biscuits & Gravy ..... 8
Air Fryer Sausage Patties ..... 9
Air Fryer Pancake Muffins ..... 9
Air Fryer Bacon Wrapped Avocados ..... 10
Air Fryer Omelette ..... 10
Air-Fryer Breakfast Croquettes With Egg And Asparagus ..... 11
Air Fryer Scrambled Eggs ..... 11
Air Fryer Breakfast Egg Wraps ..... 12
Air Fryer Breakfast Bacon Biscuits ..... 12

CHAPTER 2: LUNCH RECIPES 13

Air Fryer Crispy Chicken Nuggets With Dip ..... 14
Air Fryer Wonton Mozzarella Sticks ..... 14
Air Fryer Quinoa And Cauliflower Steaks ..... 15
Air Fryer Prawn Fajitas ..... 15
Air Fryer Baked Steak Fries ..... 16
Air Fryer Sweet Potato Oven Fries ..... 16
Air Fryer Chicken And Broccoli ..... 17
Air Fryer Chicken Cordon Bleu ..... 17
Air Fryer Roasted Balsamic Brussels Sprouts ..... 18
Air Fryer Chili Garlic Tofu ..... 18
Air Fryer Mac 'n' Cheese ..... 19
Air Fryer Pasta Chips ..... 19
Air Fryer Kung Pao Brussels Sprouts ..... 20
Air Fryer Onion Rings ..... 20
Air Fryer Spaghetti Squash 'Pasta' ..... 21
Air Fryer Italian Meatballs ..... 21
Air Fryer Fried Rice ..... 22
Air Fryer Baked Potatoes ..... 22
Air Fryer Breaded Chicken Drumsticks ..... 23
Air Fryer Vegetable Casserole With Sausages And Bacon ..... 23
Air Fryer Chicken Alfredo With Mushrooms And Spinach ..... 24
Air Fryer Pasta Primavera ..... 24
Air Fryer Courgette Fries With Tahini Dipping Sauce ..... 25
Air Fryer Pork Loin With Potatoes And Mushrooms ..... 25
Air Fryer Coconut Pork And Green Beans ..... 26
Air Fryer Chicken Casserole ..... 26
Air Fryer Lemon Mango Chicken ..... 27
Air Fryer Pork Stuffed Bell Peppers ..... 27
Air Fryer Lamb Kebabs ..... 28
Air Fryer Lobster Tails With Garlic Butter-Lemon-Parsley Sauce ..... 28

CHAPTER 3: DINNER RECIPES 29

Air Fryer Fried Rice ..... 30
Air Fryer Whole Chicken ..... 30
Air Fryer Tilapia ..... 31
Air Fryer Salmon with Asparagus ..... 31
Air Fryer Prawns ..... 32
Air Fryer Pork Ribs ..... 32
Air Fryer Catfish ..... 33
Air Fryer Steak Bites and Mushrooms ..... 33
Air Fryer Ginger Lime Prawns ..... 34
Air Fryer Tofu with Honey Garlic Sauce ..... 34
Air Fryer Tuna Carbonara ..... 35
Air fryer Chicken Tikka Kebab ..... 35
Air fryer scallops ..... 36
Air Fryer Sous Vide Chicken ..... 36
Air fryer duck breast ..... 37
Air fryer chicken katsu ..... 37

Air Fryer Country Fried Steak ........ 38
Air fryer potato wedges ........ 38
Air Fryer Bacon-Wrapped Pork Tenderloin ........ 39
Air Fryer Jicama Fries Recipe (Chili Cheese Fries) ........ 39
Air Fried Cauliflower Wings ........ 40
Air Fryer Crispy Chicken Tenders ........ 40
Air Fryer Bacon Avocado Fries ........ 41
Air Fryer Butterflied Lemon Chicken ........ 41
Air Fryer Arancini (Rice Balls) ........ 42
Air Fryer Turkey Croquettes ........ 42
Air fryer sticky pork belly bites ........ 43
Air Fryer Fish And Sweet Potato Chips ........ 43
Air Fryer Fish Tacos ........ 44
Air Fryer Spinach And Feta Quiche ........ 44

## CHAPTER 4: SNACK RECIPES 45

Air Fryer Spiced Chickpeas ........ 46
Air Fryer Baked Oatmeal ........ 46
Air Fryer Courgette Chips ........ 47
Air Fryer Potato Chips ........ 47
Air Fryer Sugary Pecans ........ 48
Air Fryer Baba Ganoush ........ 48
Air Fryer Hot Pickle Chips ........ 49
Air Fryer Ham And Cheese Crescent Rolls ........ 49
Air Fryer Steak Jerky ........ 50
Air Fryer Sweet Wontons ........ 50
Air Fryer Cottage Fries ........ 51
Air Fryer Hush Puppies ........ 51
Air Fryer Buffalo Cauliflower Bites ........ 52
Air Fryer Mozzarella Sticks with Marinara & Sun-Dried Tomato ........ 52
Air Fryer Toasted Ravioli ........ 53
Air Fryer Spanakopita Bites ........ 53
Air Fryer Nachos ........ 54
Air Fryer Chicken and Hummus Stew ........ 54
Air Fryer Cheese Breadsticks ........ 55
Air Fryer Baked Onion Rings ........ 55

## CHAPTER 5: DESSERT RECIPES 56

Air Fryer Lava Cakes ........ 57
Air Fryer Baked Apples ........ 57
Air Fryer Chocolate Chip Biscuits ........ 58
Air Fryer Carrot Cake ........ 58
Air Fryer Banana Bread ........ 59
Air Fryer Cinnamon Sugar Dessert Fries ........ 59
Air Fryer Pumpkin Pie Twists ........ 60
Air Fryer Pineapple Upside-Down Cake ........ 60
Air Fryer Strawberry Nutella Hand Pies ........ 61
Air Fryer Peanut Butter Banana Energy Bites ........ 61
Air Fryer Pumpkin Applesauce Muffins ........ 62
Air Fryer Twix Cheesecake ........ 62
Air Fryer Oreos ........ 63
Air Fryer Bananas Foster ........ 63
Air Fryer Banana Pudding ........ 64
Air Fryer Donuts ........ 64
Air Fryer Apple Fritters ........ 65
Air Fryer Yogurt and Fruit Pie ........ 65
Air Fryer Beignets ........ 66
Air Fryer Grilled Peaches ........ 66

# INTRODUCTION

In 2011 I saw an air fryer at a friend's house and I was intrigued. I had never even seen one before! At the time, I was overweight and unhealthy. I was trying to figure out how to cook healthier but still eat what I liked. I decided to buy an air fryer and try it out. I loved the idea, but there was one problem. I didn't know where to start!

I began with basic fries and made a ton of them, thinking it was going to be easy and I would be able to learn the rest real quick. Well, it turned out to be the hardest part of making air fryer recipes. After several unsuccessful attempts at making fried foods, I gave up on making anything else and just focused on desserts using my new-found cooking method. I liked the desserts.

One day I tried some chicken wings at a restaurant and they were so good. That is when I found out they were cooked in an air fryer. My mind was blown! So I decided to give it another try, this time just making wings. The first attempt was much better than my first attempts at fries, but still not good enough to share with anyone else.

I continued practicing and experimenting with making fried foods until I finally got it right. My family and friends loved my new way of cooking but I was still frustrated because I was convinced it wasn't possible to make fried food without having them taste like burnt grease. So I kept practicing until I found the right balance of ingredients, breading, and cooking times. After a lot of trial and error, I finally figured out a way to make air fryer recipes that tasted great.

Why am I telling you all of this? Because I don't want you to have to go through what I went through just to get started with air fryer recipes.

My new mission in life was to share my discovery with the world. I wanted to let the world know about it and make the world a healthier place. I thought that if my discovery could help one person, then my mission would have been a success.

But now I have learned that my discovery isn't just going to help one person; it is going to help millions. That is why I wrote this book. I want to give you a step-by-step guide to making air fryer recipes so that you can enjoy cooking healthier. I want to take the mystery out of making air fryer recipes.

In this book, I am going to show you everything from delicious desserts to savory french fries, from snacks to main dishes. All of my air fryer recipe creations will be in here! The best part is that you don't have to be a chef, just look at the ingredients and cooking instructions and you will have a successful recipe.

The ingredients are all easy to find and affordable, so it won't break the bank! And don't worry about making any mistakes or burning things, because I cover every detail of each recipe so that you know exactly what to do.

If you aren't sure where to start, just flip through the pages and see what your friends and family like. Then try something different the next time you make it and see if they liked it more. It is all about experimenting.

I hope you find the book helpful and that you enjoy these delicious recipes.

# CHAPTER 1: BREAKFAST RECIPES

## Air Fryer Breakfast Pizza

**Prep Time: 5 minutes | Cook Time: 20 minutes | Serves 4**

190 g frozen shredded hash browns
120 ml pizza sauce
225 g mozzarella cheese
2 eggs
95 g cooked bacon, crumbled
120 ml ketchup or barbecue sauce

1. Preheat your air fryer to 180°C for 10 minutes.
2. Microwave the hash browns for about 1-2 minutes to thaw them.
3. Place the hash browns in a large bowl and mix in the pizza sauce, mozzarella cheese, eggs and bacon.
4. Pour into your air fryer basket and cook for 20 minutes at 180°C or until golden brown with a crispy exterior and soft center.
5. Top with ketchup or barbecue sauce and serve.

## Air Fryer Banana Bread

**Prep Time: 5 minutes | Cook Time: 25 minutes | Serves 4**

225 g granulated sugar
110 ml butter or margarine, melted
1 egg
225 g plain flour
4 g baking powder
5 g salt
6 g cinnamon powder
200 g thick bananas, mashed

1. Preheat your air fryer to 185°C for 10 minutes.
2. In a large bowl, mix together the sugar on melted butter or margarine, until combined. Add in the egg and mix until combined.
3. In another bowl, mix together the flour, baking powder, salt and cinnamon. Pour the dry mixture into the wet mixture and mix until combined.
4. Fold in the mashed bananas with a spatula or spoon until combined. Grease a loaf tin of your choice with butter or oil then pour in the banana bread mixture (it will be very sticky).
5. Cook for 20 minutes at 185°C or until a toothpick comes out clean. Cool for 5 minutes in the air fryer before turning onto a wire rack to cool completely. Serve and enjoy.

# Air Fryer Crispy Breakfast Burritos

**Prep Time: 15 minutes | Cook Time: 30 minutes | Serves 6**

6 large eggs
120g black beans
4g chopped cilantro
20g fresh cheese, grated
30ml olive oil
6 small tortillas
5g red onion, thinly sliced
500g potatoes

1. Preheat the air fryer to 180ºC
2. In a large bowl, whisk together the eggs, beans and cilantro until combined. Pour the egg mixture into a skillet sprayed lightly with olive oil cooking spray over medium heat and cook for 1-2 minutes until starting to set.
3. Sprinkle the grated cheese evenly over the top of the mixture and cook for 30 seconds until melted through, then flip it over and cook until just cooked through; remove from the heat and set aside.
4. Place half the mixture on each tortilla and roll up, then place the burritos seam-side down in a baking dish sprayed lightly with olive oil cooking spray.
5. Slice the potatoes into bite-sized pieces and add them to the baking dish with the burritos, then drizzle with olive oil and sprinkle over red onion. Air fry for 8 minutes until golden brown
6. Serve immediately.

# Air fryer Monkey Bread

**Prep Time: 5 minutes | Cook Time: 25 minutes | Serves 4**

225 g can refrigerated biscuits
100 g unsalted butter, melted
110 ml milk, room temperature
1 egg
2 g salt
8 g cinnamon powder

1. Preheat your air fryer to 185°C for 10 minutes.
2. In a bowl, mix the biscuits with the melted butter and milk until no dry pieces remain.
3. Add in the egg and mix gently until combined.
4. Mix in the salt, cinnamon and then pour into a lightly greased 9x9 inch baking dish (or any pie pan).
5. Cook for 15 minutes at 185°C or until golden brown.
6. Remove from the air fryer, cool and then serve.

# Air Fryer Breakfast Frittata

**Prep Time: 5 minutes | Cook Time: 25 minutes | Serves 8**

225 g frozen yellow corn kernels (thawed)
300 ml can of tomato sauce
180 ml sour cream, room temperature
4 eggs
4.5 g salt
2 g black pepper powder

1. In a bowl, mix the corn kernels with the tomato sauce and sour cream. Stir to combine until well combined.
2. Add in the eggs and mix until combined. You may need to use your hands to make sure everything is mixed together well. Make sure to season well before cooking.
3. Add in any extra ingredients if desired and pour into your air fryer basket, cooking for 15 minutes at 185°C. If the base of the air fryer is too hot to touch, increase the temperature by 5 degrees. If it is too cool, reduce it by 5 degrees.
4. Allow to cool slightly before serving.

# Air Fryer French Toast

**Prep Time: 5 minutes | Cook Time: 20 minutes | Serves 4**

180 ml milk, whole
4 eggs
2 g vanilla extract
0.5 g salt
3 g cinnamon powder

1. In a bowl, whisk together the eggs, milk, vanilla extract and 0.5g of salt until well combined.
2. Add in any extra ingredients if desired and pour into your air fryer basket, cooking for 10 minutes at 180°C or until a toothpick comes out clean. If the base of the air fryer is too hot to touch, increase the temperature by 5 degrees. If it is too cool, reduce it by 5 degrees.
3. Allow to cool slightly before serving.
4. Serve and enjoy.

## Air Fryer Breakfast Potatoes

**Prep Time: 5 minutes | Cook Time: 20 minutes | Serves 4**

225 g frozen yellow corn kernels (thawed)
300 ml can of tomato sauce
140 g diced bacon, cooked and crumbled
60 g thinly sliced potatoes, cut into 1/2-inch strips
3 g salt
10 g cinnamon powder

1. In a bowl, mix the corn kernels with the tomato sauce and sour cream. Stir to combine until well combined. Add in the bacon and mix gently. Add in the sliced potatoes and stir until combined.
2. Add the salt, cinnamon and then pour into a lightly greased 9x9 inch baking dish
3. Cook for 20 minutes at 180°C or until hot and golden brown.
4. Remove from the air fryer, allow to cool slightly before serving with sour cream, bacon bits or avocado if desired.

## Air Fryer Cinnamon French Toast

**Prep Time: 5 minutes | Cook Time: 10 minutes | Serves 6**

4 eggs
2 g vanilla extract
0.5 g salt or to taste
1 g cinnamon powder

1. In a bowl, whisk together the eggs, vanilla extract and 0.5g of salt until well combined.
2. Add in any extra ingredients if desired and pour into your air fryer basket, cooking for 10 minutes at 180°C or until a toothpick comes out clean. If the base of the air fryer is too hot to touch, increase the temperature by 5 degrees. If it is too cool, reduce it by 5 degrees.
3. Allow to cool slightly before serving.

# Air Fryer Fried Simple Eggs

**Prep Time: 4 minutes | Cook Time: 6 minutes | Serves 2**

2 eggs, whisked or to taste
1 g salt or to taste
2 g pepper powder or to taste

1. Preheat your air fryer to 175°C for 10 minutes.
2. Add the egg into your air fryer basket and leave for 5 minutes or until cooked to desired firmness.
3. Remove from the air fryer, season with salt and pepper before serving.

# Air Fryer Apple Pie Egg Rolls

**Prep Time: 4 minutes | Cook Time: 6 minutes | Serves 2**

2 eggs, whisked or to taste
1.5 g salt or to taste
1 g pepper powder or to taste
2.5 g flour for egg
roll wrappers
100 g grated apple
5 g sugar
0.5 g cinnamon powder

1. Preheat your air fryer to 200°C for 10 minutes.
2. In a bowl, mix the eggs, salt and pepper until well combined then stir in the grated apple.
3. Add in any extra ingredients if desired and mix until a thick dough forms.
4. Take out an egg roll wrapper, place the mixture in it then brush around the edges with a little water before rolling up into a log shape, sealing the edges with water if needed. Repeat this process two more times.
5. Place the rolls into your air fryer basket and leave for 6 minutes at 200°C or until they are golden brown on the outside yet soft on the inside. Serve with dipping sauce if desired.

## Air Fryer Pancakes

**Prep Time: 2 minutes | Cook Time: 6 minutes | Serves 2**

150 g self-raising flour or to taste
1.5 g salt
1.5 g baking powder
1.5 g bicarbonate of soda
4 ml melted butter
4 ml milk for pancakes

1. Preheat your air fryer to 200°C for 10 minutes.
2. In a bowl, mix the butter and milk until well combined then add in any extra ingredients such as any extra eggs, sweetener etc. if desired.
3. Add in the flour, salt, baking powder and bicarbonate of soda until you have a thick batter that's easy to spread.
4. In a separate bowl, whisk your egg then add in to the batter along with any extra ingredients such as sweetener if desired then mix until well combined.
5. Place the mixture into your air fryer basket and leave for 5 minutes or until cooked. Flip over after 3 minutes.
6. Serve with maple syrup if desired.

## Air Fryer Biscuits & Gravy

**Prep Time: 2 minutes | Cook Time: 10 minutes | Serves 2**

2 eggs
15 ml milk
1 g salt
8 ml melted butter
2 g pepper powder
1 g paprika powder

1. In a bowl, mix together the eggs, salt and pepper until well combined then stir in the milk and melted butter until well combined.
2. Add in any extra ingredients if desired and mix until a thick dough forms then roll out into your desired shape such as rounds if using a cutter or small balls if using a spoon etc.
3. Place the pieces in your air fryer basket and cook for 8 minutes at 200°C.
4. Serve with your favorite gravy if desired.

## Air Fryer Sausage Patties

**Prep Time: 3 minutes | Cook Time: 10 minutes | Serves 2**

1 g salt
1.5 g pepper powder
1 egg
30 ml water
30 ml milk, heated
12 g bread crumbs, heated
110 g shredded sausages

1. In a bowl, mix the eggs and water until well combined then stir in the milk and any extra ingredients such as extra salt if desired.
2. Add in the salt and egg then mix until a thick dough forms.
3. In another bowl, add in the bread crumbs and heat in the microwave for 30 seconds before stirring through the dough then place back into your air fryer basket.
4. Cook at 200°C for 8 minutes or until cooked through or until golden brown on top before removing to serve with your favorite gravy if desired.

## Air Fryer Pancake Muffins

**Prep Time: 5 minutes | Cook Time: 10 minutes | Serves 12**

1 g salt
2 g pepper powder
1.5 g baking powder
1.5 g vanilla powder
3 ml honey or to taste
4 ml melted butter
4 ml water
100 g self-raising flour

1. Preheat your air fryer to 200°C for 10 minutes. Add in a rack if desired.
2. In a bowl, mix together the salt, baking powder and bicarbonate of soda then add in any extra ingredients such as sweetener if desired before mixing until well combined. Set aside.
3. Add in the honey or melted butter along with any extra ingredients such as extra vanilla if desired then mix until well combined.
4. Add in the water and mix until a thick dough forms. Add in your flour and mix until a thick dough forms if using self-raising flour or a thick batter if using almond flour.
5. Place the mixture into your air fryer basket and leave for 8 minutes or until cooked through and golden brown on top before removing to serve with your favorite syrup if desired.

## Air Fryer Bacon Wrapped Avocados

**Prep Time: 3 minutes | Cook Time: 7 minutes | Serves 2**

195 g avocado
3 g bacon

1. Peel the avocado then slice in half and remove the pit.
2. Remove the seed and grate over a bowl to remove any excess flesh.
3. Wrap each half of the avocado in bacon making sure to wrap all around the inside.
4. Place into your air fryer basket and cook for 6 minutes at 200°C or until golden brown on top before removing to serve with your favorite syrup if desired.

## Air Fryer Omelette

**Prep Time: 10 minutes | Cook time: 15 minutes | Serves 4**

4 eggs
100 g green onion, chopped
6 g minced garlic
28 g parsley, chopped
28 g tomatoes, diced
4 g salt
6 ml black pepper

1. In a bowl, whisk together eggs and milk. Add all other ingredients and mix well. This is your omelette batter.
2. Pour oil into the air fryer basket to a depth of 0.5-1cm
3. Using a wooden spoon, spread omelette batter evenly across the bottom of the basket without crowding.
4. Put basket into the air fryer and cook on low heat for 15 minutes. Take out and serve on a plate with a drizzle of tomato sauce or salsa.

# Air-Fryer Breakfast Croquettes With Egg And Asparagus

**Prep Time: 15 minutes | Cook Time: 15 minutes | Serves 4**

600g asparagus, trimmed, peeled and cut into 1cm pieces
115ml water
2g fresh rosemary, finely chopped
2g fresh thyme, finely chopped
3g garlic powder
3g salt
3g black pepper
2 large eggs, beaten
120g whole-wheat flour
30ml olive oil
60g brown sugar, packed
6ml vanilla extract

1. Preheat the air fryer to 240ºC.
2. In a large bowl, mix together the flour and baking powder; stir in the oil and brown sugar until evenly combined.
3. Add the eggs and vanilla extract; stir to combine until just combined and no lumps remain.
4. Add the chopped asparagus, chopped rosemary, chopped thyme, garlic powder, salt and black pepper; stir to combine until evenly distributed throughout the batter.
5. Spread the batter in a single layer over a paper towel-lined plate and bake for 10-15 minutes until golden brown.
6. Serve immediately.

# Air Fryer Scrambled Eggs

**Prep Time: 10 minutes | Cook Time: 5 minutes | Serves 2**

2 eggs
2.5 g butter
2.5 g salt
2.5 g black pepper

1. Put eggs in a pan and cover with cold water by about an inch or so (about two inches for bigger eggs).
2. Over medium-high heat, bring water to a boil.
3. As soon as the water is boiling, cover the saucepan and remove from heat. Let stand for ten minutes.
4. Drain the hot water and run cold tap water over the eggs until they are room temperature.
5. Put eggs in a bowl; add butter, salt and pepper. Whisk together.
6. Put egg mixture into the air fryer. Cook on high for four minutes.
7. When the scrambled egg is done cooking, add cheese to the top and then fold it in half with a spatula.

# Air Fryer Breakfast Egg Wraps

**Prep Time: 10 minutes | Cook Time: 10 minutes | Serves 4**

2 eggs
250 g bacon, cooked and crumbled
1.5 g salt
0.5 g black pepper

1. Put eggs in a pan and cover with cold water by about an inch or so (about two inches for bigger eggs)
2. Over medium-high heat, bring water to a boil
3. As soon as the water is boiling, cover the saucepan and remove from heat. Let stand for ten minutes.
4. Drain the hot water and run cold tap water over the eggs until they are room temperature.
5. Put eggs in a bowl; add bacon, salt and pepper. Whisk together.
6. Spread egg mixture on a tortilla (flatbread). Roll up tortilla. Cut in half before serving or into fourths to serve with salsa (a tomato-based sauce).
7. Enjoy with coffee or tea.

# Air Fryer Breakfast Bacon Biscuits

**Prep Time: 15 minutes | Cook Time: 15 minutes | Serves 4**

120g bacon - streaky chopped
125g pecan nuts, roughly chopped
100g whole-wheat flour
25g brown sugar, packed
1g baking powder
30ml olive oil
4g chopped chives
5g Dijon mustard
3ml lemon juice

1. Preheat the air fryer to 270ºC.
2. In a large bowl, mix together the flour, baking powder and chopped chives until evenly combined.
3. In a large skillet sprayed lightly with olive oil cooking spray over medium heat cook the bacon until crispy, and then add the chopped pecans; cook until fragrant.
4. Add the flour mixture; stir to combine until well combined and starting to come together.
5. Pour the batter into parchment paper baking cups and pipe small amounts onto the biscuit sheets.
6. Bake for 10-15 minutes or until golden brown; serve immediately.

# CHAPTER 2: LUNCH RECIPES

## Air Fryer Crispy Chicken Nuggets With Dip

**Prep Time: 15 minutes | Cook Time: 10 minutes | Serves 2**

20 g unsalted butter, melted
450 g chicken breasts, skinless, thinly sliced
3 g garlic, finely minced
2 g salt
2 g Fresh parsley, chopped
4 g black pepper
40 ml low-fat mayonnaise
10 ml white balsamic vinegar or apple cider vinegar

1. Heat your air fryer to 180°C and place the basket inside of it.
2. In a large bowl, combine the mayonnaise with vinegar, parsley, salt and pepper. Whisk it well.
3. Now lay the chicken breasts in a single layer in the basket of your air fryer and cook for 8 minutes at 160°C. Place a stick of butter on each chicken breast during cooking to make it more tender.
4. After eight minutes, take your chicken breasts out of the basket and give it a dip in the sauce.

## Air Fryer Wonton Mozzarella Sticks

**Prep Time: 15 minutes | Cook Time: 5 minutes | Serves 1**

1.5 g salt
15 g Panko breadcrumbs
60 g egg white
2 g pepper
22 g Parmesan cheese, grated
10 ml olive oil

1. Place the wontons in a single layer in the basket of your air fryer and cook for 3 minutes at 170 °C. While your wontons are getting ready, beat the egg whites with salt and pepper. Add the Parmesan cheese in two or three installments.
2. In the next step, dip the cooked wontons in the beaten egg whites and then roll in the Panko breadcrumbs. Put them back in the basket of your air fryer and cook until golden brown on both sides.

# Air Fryer Quinoa And Cauliflower Steaks

**Prep Time: 15 minutes | Cook Time: 10 minutes| Serves 4**

4 g lemon, squeezed
10 ml olive oil
2 g Dijon mustard
2 g honey
1.5 g salt
20 g Parmesan cheese, grated
500 g quinoa, cooked and cooled
15 ml balsamic vinegar or apple cider vinegar
450 g cauliflower, cut into florets and stems sliced

1. Mix the lemon zest with the Dijon mustard, honey, salt and Parmesan cheese. Heat your air fryer to 200 °C.
2. In a large bowl, combine the cooked quinoa with the vinegar and the lemon mixture and then add the cauliflower stems and florets. Give it a stir to get them nicely coated in all of its flavors.
3. Once combined, transfer the mixture to an air fryer and cook for about 10 minutes. Once it is done, take it out of the oven and garnish with chopped parsley.
4. Simultaneously, in a small bowl add the egg whites with the milk and beat until smooth. Pour into prepared pan over the cauliflower and stir gently to combine everything well together.

# Air Fryer Prawn Fajitas

**Prep Time: 15 minutes | Cook Time: 5 minutes | Serves 2**

4 g chili flakes
1 g salt
2 g dried red chili pepper, in slices
45 ml olive oil
1.5 g garlic, minced
20 g fresh parsley, chopped
1.5 g cumin powder
450 g prawn, peeled and deveined
20 ml lemon juice or pineapple juice (optional)
3 ml honey (optional)

1. Season your prawn with the chili flakes, salt and cumin. In a large bowl, stir together the olive oil and the garlic. Then add the parsley, honey and lemon or pineapple juice. If you have chosen to use this extra ingredient, then you will need a little bit more of it because it helps to tenderize the prawn.
2. Now add the prawn pieces to the bowl and stir them gently with your hand until they are evenly coated in all of its flavors. Place the prawn in a single layer in the basket of your air fryer and cook for 3 minutes at 160 °C. When the prawn are done, take them out of the oven and distribute them around layers of lettuce leaves.
3. Drizzle with a little bit extra lemon juice if you would like to add extra flavor to your dish.

## Air Fryer Baked Steak Fries

**Prep Time: 15 minutes | Cook Time: 15 minutes | Serves 2**

1 g salt
450 g steak fries or sweet potatoes, cut into wedges and peeled if desired (yams are also good)
2 g paprika powder, sweet or smoked
25 ml olive oil, extra virgin

1. Preheat your Air Fryer to 190 °C. Then combine the olive oil with the paprika powder.
2. Spread the fries in a single layer in the basket of your air fryer and cook for about 15 minutes at 190 °C. If you would like a crunchier steak fry, then cook it for a shorter time.

## Air Fryer Sweet Potato Oven Fries

**Prep Time: 5 minutes | Cook Time: 18 minutes | Serves 2**

450 g sweet potato, cut into wedges
2 g garlic, minced
2 g rosemary, finely chopped
1.5 g salt
1.5 g pepper
30 ml olive oil

1. In a large bowl, combine the olive oil with the rosemary and garlic. Now add the sweet potato and stir to evenly coat each piece with its flavors.
2. Add some salt and pepper to your dish as well if you would like more flavor. Mix everything together until everything is well coated in all of its flavors.
3. Preheat your air fryer to 180 °C and spread the sweet potato wedges in a single layer in the basket of your air fryer. Cook it for 18 minutes at 180 °C.
4. Take them out and garnish with plenty of chopped parsley if you like.

# Air Fryer Chicken And Broccoli

**Prep Time: 15 minutes | Cook Time: 11 minutes | Serves 4**

2 g pepper, freshly ground
15 ml olive oil, extra virgin
450 g chicken breast fillets (skinless and boneless) cut into smaller pieces (or other pieces of chicken you would like to prepare)
180 g rice
3.5 g butter or margarine
2 g garlic, minced
1.5 g pepper
2 g salt (or to taste)
200 g broccoli florets (fresh or frozen)

1. In a large bowl, pour the olive oil and add the chicken pieces with salt and pepper to your taste. Then add the broccoli and toss everything together until they are well coated with its flavor.
2. Preheat your air fryer to 190 °C.
3. In a small bowl, add the butter or margarine and the garlic and pepper. Cover the bowl and allow it to stand for 10 minutes in order for the flavors to become stronger.
4. Add the chicken mixture to your air fryer basket, followed by the rice and half of your butter or margarine mixture. Stir everything until it is evenly coated with all its flavors.
5. Cook for 11 minutes at 190 °C. Take it out and serve with your remaining butter or margarine mixture over the top and garnish with plenty of freshly chopped parsley.

# Air Fryer Chicken Cordon Bleu

**Prep Time: 15 minutes | Cook Time: 10 minutes | Serves 4**

2.5 g salt
3.5 g pepper
300 g chicken breast fillets (skinless and boneless)
2.5 g garlic powder or fresh garlic chopped
1.5 g onion powder
2 g paprika powder
200 g thick cut bacon (unsalted)
150 g ham, sliced
2.5 g parsley, finely chopped
3 g egg whisked
4 g all-purpose flour

1. In a large bowl, add the garlic powder, onion powder, salt and pepper to your taste. Then add the chicken breast fillets with all of its juices and mix it carefully until they are evenly coated with its flavors. If you would like your chicken to be really tender then you should allow them to sit in the fridge for at least an hour before cooking.
2. Preheat your air fryer to 190 °C.
3. In a large bowl, add the eggs and whisk them thoroughly until they are smooth. On one side of the chicken breast, place a slice of ham followed by a slice of bacon on top. Roll it carefully until it is tightly wrapped around your chicken breast and secure it with a toothpick.
4. Flour your air fryer basket with some flour and then gently place the wrapped chicken inside the basket. Cook for 10 minutes at 190 °C. Take them out and slice them into thick slices before serving.

# Air Fryer Roasted Balsamic Brussels Sprouts

**Prep Time: 15 minutes | Cook Time: 15 minutes | Serves 3**

450 g Brussels sprouts, trimmed and halved lengthwise
1.5 g paprika powder
3 g garlic, chopped or grated
2.5 g salt
2.5 g pepper
100 ml olive oil

1. Preheat your air fryer to 190°C.
2. In a small bowl, pour the olive oil and add the garlic, paprika and salt and pepper to your taste. Mix everything together until all ingredients are well blended, set aside.
3. Spread the Brussels sprouts onto your air fryer basket, making sure that they are evenly spread around the bottom of the basket so it cooks evenly.
4. Cook for 15 minutes at 190 °C.
5. Take them out and serve warm with the balsamic vinaigrette over the top.

# Air Fryer Chili Garlic Tofu

**Prep Time: 15 minutes | Cook Time: 10 minutes | Serves 2-3**

1 g garlic powder
500 g tofu, drained and pressed (make sure its pressed well before cooking)
1.5 g paprika powder
3.5 g salt
1.5 g pepper
1 g red chilli, finely chopped (optional)
100 ml olive oil

1. Preheat your air fryer to 190 °C.
2. In a large bowl, pour the olive oil and add the garlic powder, paprika powder and season with salt and pepper to your taste before tossing it through the tofu. Make sure that you toss it well so all of the spices get evenly coated on top of your tofu.
3. Place the tofu onto your air fryer basket and cook for 10 minutes at 190 °C.
4. Take out of the air fryer and divide into serving sizes.
5. Top with some chopped red chilli and serve warm.

## Air Fryer Mac ‘n’ Cheese

**Prep Time: 10 minutes | Cook Time: 10 minutes | Serves 3**

1.5 g salt
2 g black pepper
3.5 g garlic, finely chopped or grated
1.5 g cayenne pepper (optional but you can add more if desired)
500 g macaroni pasta
600 ml whole milk
1.5 g mustard powder (optional)
3 eggs, whisked together
15 g butter, melted

1. Preheat your air fryer to 190 °C.
2. In a medium sized bowl, place the black pepper, paprika powder, salt and cayenne pepper (if using). Mix everything together until it is evenly distributed. Then add the macaroni pasta and mix well together so that all of the spices get evenly distributed throughout it.
3. Whisk the milk, mustard powder and eggs together in a separate bowl and add it to your macaroni pasta until it is well mixed.
4. Place half of the macaroni pasta onto your air fryer basket and cook for 10 minutes at 190 °C. Take them out and serve warm with the cheese sauce, breadcrumbs and grated parmesan over the top.

## Air Fryer Pasta Chips

**Prep Time: 15 minutes | Cook Time: 20 minutes | Serves 3**

500 g deep fry pasta, dried
1.5 g salt
1.5 g pepper
3.5 g garlic powder or grated garlic
500 ml vegetable broth

1. In a large bowl, add the salt, pepper and garlic powder and mix everything together until well combined. Then add the pasta and mix until they are well coated with it’s spices. Let it sit in the fridge for at least an hour so that it is fully marinated with its spices.
2. Preheat your air fryer to 190 °C.
3. Place half of the pasta onto your air fryer basket and cook for 15 minutes at 190 °C.
4. Take them out and place them onto your baking tray with a baking paper on top. Place another baking paper on top and press gently to ensure that it sticks together well and form into a single layer.
5. Repeat step 3 with the remaining pasta until it is cooked at 190 °C. Allow the pasta to cool and then break the single layer into smaller pieces and store in an airtight container to keep it fresh.

# Air Fryer Kung Pao Brussels Sprouts

**Prep Time: 10 minutes | Cook Time: 12 minutes | Serves 1**

2 g garlic powder
2.5 g fresh ginger, finely chopped
1.5 g salt
1.5 g red chilli, finely chopped (optional)
1.5 g black pepper
1.5 g ground coriander
1.5 g paprika powder
140 g Brussels sprouts, halved

1. In a large bowl, pour the olive oil and add the garlic powder, salt, red chilli (if using), black pepper and ground coriander to your taste.
2. Toss everything together until it is evenly coated with its flavors and add the Brussels sprouts. Make sure that you toss them thoroughly so all of its spices get evenly distributed throughout them
3. Preheat your air fryer to 190 °C.
4. Place half of the Brussels sprouts onto your air fryer basket and cook for 12 minutes at 190 °C.
5. Take them out and serve warm with some crumbled crispy baked tofu if you wish on top.

# Air Fryer Onion Rings

**Prep Time: 12 minutes | Cook Time: 12 minutes | Serves 2**

500 g onion, thinly sliced
20 g cornflake crumbs or breadcrumbs (optional)
1.5 g fresh parsley, finely chopped
3.5 g fresh thyme, finely chopped
1.5 g salt
1.5 g pepper

1. Preheat your air fryer to 190 °C.
2. In a medium sized bowl, place the cornflake crumbs or breadcrumbs (optional), salt, pepper and thyme and mix everything together until it is evenly distributed.
3. Pour the olive oil into a separate bowl and add the parsley before mixing them together. Mix well until it is evenly distributed through it.
4. Pour the oil into a third bowl and mix everything together well before toss it through the onion rings.
5. Place half of the onion rings onto your air fryer basket and cook for 12 minutes at 190 °C.
6. Take them out and serve warm along with some ketchup if you wish on top.

## Air Fryer Spaghetti Squash 'Pasta'

**Prep Time: 10 minutes | Cook Time: 17 minutes | Serves 2-3**

500 g spaghetti squash, cooked, scooped out and halved
1.5 g salt
2 egg yolks, whisked well together (optional)
1.5 g pepper
3.5 g garlic powder or grated garlic (optional)

1. Preheat your air fryer to 190 °C.
2. On a baking tray, place the spaghetti squash halves side by side and drizzle with olive oil and sprinkle with its spices.
3. Bake in the air fryer for 15 minutes at 190 °C.
4. Take out of the oven and allow it to cool before scooping out the seeds inside it and mixing them into small balls.
5. Place half of the spaghetti squash 'pasta' onto your air fryer basket and cook for 2 minutes at 190 °C. Take them out and serve warm with some cheese sauce on top if you wish.

## Air Fryer Italian Meatballs

**Prep Time: 10 minutes | Cook Time: 15 minutes | Serves 4**

1 kg minced beef or pork
2 g basil, finely chopped (optional)
2 g garlic powder
1.5 g salt
1.5 g pepper (optional)

1. Preheat your air fryer to 190 °C.
2. In a medium sized bowl, add the minced beef or pork with the basil, garlic powder and salt and mix everything together until it is evenly distributed in it.
3. In a third medium sized bowl, place the egg yolks and whisk them well together before mixing them into the meat mixture.
4. Place half of the meatballs over your air fryer basket and cook for 15 minutes at 190 °C.
5. Once done, take them out and serve warm with some spaghetti sauce on top if you wish.

# Air Fryer Fried Rice

**Prep Time: 10 minutes | Cook Time: 10 minutes | Serves 4**

500 g white or brown rice (cooked)
5 g garlic powder
5 g fresh ginger
2.5 g turmeric powder
3 g salt
200 g carrots, diced
20 ml olive oil (or canola oil)
2 g pepper

1. Take a mixing bowl, combine all rice ingredients in there, then add the olive oil and pepper. Mix it all together. Preheat the air fryer to 200 °C.
2. Once you're done preheating, add the rice mixture into the basket of your air fryer and cook it for 10 minutes at 200 °C
3. After 10 minutes, add more oil and pepper if desired
4. Once you're done cooking your dish, let it cool completely. Serve!

# Air Fryer Baked Potatoes

**Prep Time: 10 minutes | Cook Time: 20 minutes | Serves 3**

450 g white potatoes (peeled and cubed)
150 g butter (unsalted)
50 ml sour cream or mayonnaise (or to taste)
2.5 g salt
1.5 g black pepper
5 g paprika powder

1. Take a baking dish, then place potatoes inside the dish.
2. Take a small bowl and mix sour cream with butter, salt, pepper and paprika powder. Then pour this mixture into the dish with potatoes.
3. Put the basket of your air fryer on top of the baking dish which contains potatoes and pour 200ml water inside your air fryer. Cook it for 20 minutes at 200 °C.
4. Once you're done cooking your dish, let it cool completely and serve.

## Air Fryer Breaded Chicken Drumsticks

**Prep Time: 15 minutes | Cook Time: 6 minutes | Serves 1**

250 g chicken drumsticks
1.5 g salt
1.5 g black pepper
2.5 g paprika powder
25 ml vegetable oil (or canola oil)

1. Mix chicken seasoning with a pinch of salt and the black pepper, then shake it all together in a bowl. Make sure you don't over-blend these ingredients because the seasoning should retain its shape when you shake it up well.
2. Preheat the air fryer to 200 °C. Put the chicken drumsticks in a bowl and coat the drumsticks with the seasoning you just made.
3. Add the oil to a heat-proof plate then put it inside your air fryer basket and cook it for 3 minutes at 200 °C.
4. After 3 minutes (or when the oil starts to smoke), take the drumsticks out of your air fryer. Then put the drumsticks on a plate and cover it with foil.
5. Add salt and paprika powder to the same oil in step 3 and heat it up again for 2 minutes at 200 °C. Then cook the drumstick again for 30 seconds at 200 °C to finish it off. Serve it with a dipping sauce like ketchup or marinara sauce.

## Air Fryer Vegetable Casserole With Sausages And Bacon

**Prep Time: 3 minutes | Cook Time: 40 minutes | Serves 2**

80 ml olive oil (or canola oil)
200 g potatoes
60 ml milk
10 ml lemon juice
5 g garlic powder
1.5 g salt
300 g sausages (any type of sausage you want)
40 g bacon (cut into thin slices)

1. Place a baking dish inside the air fryer basket and pour in 150ml water.
2. Add potatoes to the basket of the air fryer and cook it for 20 minutes at 200 °C.
3. After 20 minutes, add oil and garlic. Cook it for 5 minutes at 200 °C then add milk and lemon juice, cook it for 5 more minutes at 200 °C, then add sausage and bacon to the air fryer and cook it for 10 more minutes at 200 °C.
4. Serve it with ketchup or BBQ sauce.

# Air Fryer Chicken Alfredo With Mushrooms And Spinach

**Prep Time: 35 minutes | Cook Time: 15 minutes | Serves 8**

1.5 kg cooked skinless chicken breasts and thighs (cut into bite-sized pieces)
500 g mushrooms (sliced)
1000 ml hundred per cent vegetable saffron sauce
20 g unsalted butter, melted
5 ml lemon juice
200 g spinach (fresh or frozen)
1.5 g salt
1.5 g black pepper

1. Put the chicken, mushrooms and spinach in a mixing bowl.
2. Put the saffron sauce in a saucepan and bring it to a simmer over medium heat. Add the butter and lemon juice, then whizz well until frothy. Pour into the mixing bowl with mushrooms and spinach with chicken.
3. Season with salt & pepper then toss well to ensure all ingredients are evenly coated in sauce.
4. Place the basket of your air fryer on top of the baking dish containing the chicken and sauce, then pour 200ml water in your air fryer to prevent spills. Cook it for 15 minutes at 200 °C.
5. Serve with rice or pasta.

# Air Fryer Pasta Primavera

**Prep Time: 10 minutes | Cook Time: 6 minutes | Serves 3**

400 g mixed vegetable (sliced)
2 g salt
1.5 g black pepper
1.5 g paprika powder
70 g broccoli floret (fresh or frozen)
300 g penne pasta (cooked)
25 ml olive oil (or canola oil)

1. Put vegetable, salt, paprika and black pepper in a mixing bowl and combine well.
2. Add broccoli and penne pasta to the mixing bowl.
3. Add olive oil to a heat-proof plate then put it into your air fryer basket and cook it for 3 minutes at 200 °C.
4. After 3 minutes (or when the oil starts to smoke), take the vegetables out of your air fryer. Then add salt, pepper and paprika powder to the same oil in step 3 and heat it up again for 2 minutes at 200 °C. Then cook the vegetables again for 30 seconds at 200 °C to finish it off.
5. Serve it with ketchup or marinara sauce.

## Air Fryer Courgette Fries With Tahini Dipping Sauce

**Prep Time: 15 minutes | Cook Time: 13 minutes | Serves 2**

450 g courgette (cut into thick match sticks)
2 g salt
1.5 g black pepper
25 ml olive oil (or canola oil)
50 ml tahini sauce

1. Combine courgette, salt and black pepper in a mixing bowl.
2. Set up your air fryer basket to contain the courgette fries and pour 100ml water into it. Cook it for 5 minutes at 200 °C then take it out and drain the excess water.
3. Put the basket back into your air fryer and add oil, cook it for 5 more minutes at 200 °C.
4. After 5 minutes, take it out and drain the excess oil by holding a kitchen towel over the basket. Then add black pepper and salt to the same oil in step 3 and heat it up again for 2 minutes at 200 °C. Then cook courgette fries again for 30 seconds at 200 °C to finish it off.
5. Serve it with tahini sauce.

## Air Fryer Pork Loin With Potatoes And Mushrooms

**Prep Time: 15 minutes | Cook Time: 40 minutes | Serves 4**

700 g pork loin, smoked and/or grilled (cut into bite-sized pieces)
1 g salt
1.5 g black pepper
2 g paprika powder
300 g potatoes (sliced)
100 g white button mushrooms (sliced)
25 ml olive oil (or canola oil)

1. Preheat the air fryer at 180 °C for 5 minutes. Then mix the olive oil with the potatoes and season them with salt and pepper. Sprinkle paprika on top of the potatoes.
2. Put half of the olive oil into the basket of the air fryer and put in half of the potato pieces, then repeat using a second layer (the remaining potatoes). Bake for 20 minutes or until golden brown.
3. Meanwhile, mix the remaining olive oil with the mushrooms and season them with salt and pepper.
4. Put half of the mushrooms on top of the pork and then add a layer of potatoes. Repeat using a second layer (the remaining pork).
5. Bake for another 20 minutes at 180 °C or until golden brown.

# Air Fryer Coconut Pork And Green Beans

**Prep Time: 15 minutes | Cook Time: 30 minutes | Serves 2**

1 g salt
2.5 g pepper
150 g green beans (trimmed)
200 g pork tenderloin
(cut into strips)
2 g crushed garlic
60 ml coconut oil

1. Preheat the air fryer at 180 °C for 5 minutes.
2. Mix the pork, green bean and garlic in the bowl and season them with salt and pepper.
3. Put half of the coconut oil into the basket of the air fryer, put in half of the pork, green beans and garlic mix and repeat this step with a second layer (the remaining pork). Bake for 20 minutes or until golden brown.
4. Meanwhile, heat up a frying pan at 180 °C with coconut oil on medium heat.
5. Add the pork to the pan and season with salt and pepper. Fry until the pork is slightly brown on one side, then flip over and fry for another 5 minutes or until cooked through.
6. Remove air fryer from the heat and transfer pork to a plate.

# Air Fryer Chicken Casserole

**Prep Time: 5 minutes | Cook Time: 13 minutes | Serves 2**

1.5 g butter, unsalted
20 ml olive oil
2.5 g garlic, minced
4 g salt
2.5 g black pepper
200 g chicken breast,
cut into pieces
1.5 g parsley, chopped fine
210 ml heavy cream

1. Preheat your air fryer to 200 °C for a few minutes. Then put the butter and oil in the bowl with the chicken and mix well so the seasonings are evenly distributed. Then, bake the chicken for 7 minutes to get it right.
2. Add the parsley, garlic and seasonings to an air fryer basket and cook at 200 °C for 2 minutes. Then slice the chicken again and add it back to the basket. Bake for another 4 minutes or until you see that one side is golden brown, then remove from the oven and leave to cool a bit before serving with a side of mashed potatoes or noodles or even with rice.

## Air Fryer Lemon Mango Chicken

**Prep Time: 10 minutes | Cook Time: 50 minutes | Serves 2-3**

1.5 g salt
1.5 g black pepper
4 g garlic, minced
4 g parsley, chopped fine
2.5 ml lemon juice
1 g chili flakes
450 g skinless chicken breast, cut into pieces
40 g butter, unsalted and melted
12 g mangoes, diced
1.5 g green onions, chopped fine

1. Heat oven to 200 °C.
2. In a bowl, mix the butter with garlic, chili flakes, salt, garlic, lemon juice, parsley and seasonings. Add the chicken to the bowl and coat it in butter mixture. Bake chicken in oven for 15 minutes.
3. In a bowl, mix mangoes, melted butter and green onions together.
4. After 15 minutes, put mango mixture to an air fryer basket and bake for another 10 minutes at 200 °C.
5. After that, put the chicken back in the oven for 10 minutes 200 °C. Repeat step 3 and 4 to get additional 1-2 servings.

## Air Fryer Pork Stuffed Bell Peppers

**Prep Time: 15 minutes | Cook Time: 60 minutes | Serves 2**

1.5 g salt
1.5 g pepper
2.5 ml lemon juice or lime juice
450 g pork loin chops, cut into cubes
220 ml tomato puree (tomato sauce)
1.5 g fresh rosemary, finely chopped
2.5 ml honey (optional)

1. Season the pork with salt and pepper so it will be juicy and tasty in the end.
2. Put the pork in an air fryer basket and bake at 200 °C for 30 minutes to get it almost done.
3. Then, add the tomato puree, lemon juice, rosemary and honey (if using) and cook for another 20 minutes to get a nice brown skin on top. You can turn the heat down to 190 °C.
4. Add the pork back to the air fryer and cook for another 10 minutes at 200 °C and then remove from the oven.
5. When it's cool enough, cut into strips or cubes and enjoy.

## Air Fryer Lamb Kebabs

**Prep Time: 15 minutes | Cook Time: 55 minutes | Serves 2**

1.5 g salt
1.5 g black pepper
2.5 ml lemon juice or lime juice
450 g lamb shoulder or lamb shoulder, cut into pieces
2.5 g paprika, hot
2.5 ml honey (optional)
1 g black pepper

1. Season the lamb with salt and pepper so it will be juicy and tasty in the end.
2. Put the lamb in an air fryer basket and bake at 200 °C for 25 minutes to get it almost done. Then, add the lemon juice, paprika and honey (if using) and cook for another 20 minutes to get a nice brown skin on top. You can turn the heat down to 190 °C.
3. After that, put the lamb back in the oven for 10 minutes at 200 °C and then remove from the oven.
4. When it's cool enough, cut into pieces, top with yogurt and enjoy.

## Air Fryer Lobster Tails With Garlic Butter-Lemon-Parsley Sauce

**Prep Time: 10 minutes | Cook Time: 45 minutes | Serves 2**

1.5 g salt
1.5 g black pepper
2.5 ml lemon juice or lime juice (half of a lemon)
2.5 ml honey (optional)
480 g tail lobsters, cut into 1-inch pieces
4.5 g butter, unsalted and melted
1.5 g parsley, chopped fine (optional)

1. Season the lobster with salt and pepper so it will be juicy and tasty in the end. Put butter in an air fryer basket and bake at 200 °C for 20 minutes to get it almost done. Then add honey and lemon juice (if using) and cook for another 10 minutes to get a nice brown skin on top. You can turn the heat down to 190 °C.
2. After that, put the lobster back in the oven, add butter and parsley, cook for 15 minutes at 200 °C and then remove from the oven.
3. When it's cool enough, cut into pieces and enjoy with rice or pasta or even your favourite salad.

# CHAPTER 3: DINNER RECIPES

## Air Fryer Fried Rice

**Prep Time: 15 minutes | Cook Time: 15 minutes | Serves 2**

220 g rice, cooked much like you would cook pasta.
120 g mixed vegetables (cauliflower, carrot, peas, green beans)
100 g ground meat (optional)
2 g salt
1.5 g black pepper
2 g parsley flakes
2 g cumin powder
2 g paprika powder
2.5 g garlic powder
1.5 g onion powder
1.5 g cayenne pepper

1. Remove the rice from the cooker and place it in a large bowl to cool down for 5 minutes. Meanwhile, you can steam the mixed vegetables using a steamer for about 10 minutes. (Note: use a microwave to steam the vegetable if you do not have a steamer. They take less time to cook).
2. When the rice has cooled down, break it up by hand. Add the mixed vegetables and ground meat then drizzle in 1g of salt and mix well to combine.
3. Melt 2g of butter in a large saucepan over medium heat. Add the cumin powder, paprika powder, garlic powder, onion powder, chili flakes (optional), salt and pepper and stir well until they are well combined.
4. Add the mixture to the bowl with the rice and vegetable mixture. Mix some more and then transfer it back into the air fryer for 5 minutes at 200ºC. Remove from heat and serve with a salad.

## Air Fryer Whole Chicken

**Prep Time: 5 minutes | Cook Time: 60 minutes | Serves 8**

2.5 kg whole raw chicken
7 g black pepper
6 g onion powder
10 g garlic powder
2.5 g paprika

1. Preheat your air fryer to 180ºC.
2. Remove the neck and giblets from the chicken cavity. Pat the chicken dry.
3. Mix the black pepper, onion powder, garlic powder, and paprika in a bowl then rub it all over the chicken.
4. Place the whole chicken into the air fryer breast side down and cook for 40 minutes.
5. Flip the chicken and cook breast side up for another 15 to 20 minutes. The chicken is done when it hits 75ºC at its thickest point.
6. Remove the chicken from the air fryer, let sit for 5 minutes, then serve!

## Air Fryer Tilapia

**Prep Time: 5 minutes | Cook Time: 10 minutes | Serves 4**

4x170 g tilapia fillets
10 ml olive oil
1 g paprika
5 g garlic powder
3 g onion powder
3 g salt
3.5 black pepper
6 g lemon wedges (optional)

1. Preheat your air fryer to 200ºC.
2. Place the tilapia fillets on a large plate and drizzle with olive oil.
3. In a small bowl, mix the paprika, garlic powder, onion powder, salt, and pepper.
4. Sprinkle seasoning evenly over the fillets then place in a single layer in the air fryer.
5. Cook tilapia for 10 minutes, flipping the fillets halfway through cooking.
6. Remove the tilapia from the air fryer, serve with lemon wedges (if desired), and enjoy!

## Air Fryer Salmon with Asparagus

**Prep Time: 5 minutes | Cook Time: 10 minutes | Serves 4**

4x170 g salmon fillets
2x240 g asparagus stalks
3.5 g onion powder
5 g garlic powder
1.5 g paprika
2 g salt
1.5 g black pepper

1. Place salmon and asparagus into the air fryer in a single layer.
2. In a small bowl, mix the onion powder, garlic powder, paprika, salt, and pepper then sprinkle evenly over the salmon and asparagus. Make sure all sides are covered.
3. Cook salmon and asparagus for 10 minutes flipping halfway through cooking (or until salmon reaches 75ºC).
4. Remove from the air fryer and serve!

## Air Fryer Prawns

**Prep Time: 5 minutes | Cook Time: 10 minutes | Serves 4**

4x170 g whole prawns (on the shell)
3.5 g paprika
2 g salt
1.5 g black pepper
1.5 g onion powder
3g garlic powder
2 g lemon zest (optional)
2 g lemon juice (optional)

1. Preheat your air fryer to 200ºC. Place prawns, paprika, salt, pepper, onion powder, garlic powder, and lemon zest into the air fryer and then place them in a single layer.
2. Cook prawns and seasoning for 10 minutes flipping halfway through.
3. Remove prawns from air fryer, zest the lemon juice (if using) and serve.

## Air Fryer Pork Ribs

**Prep Time: 5 minutes | Cook Time: 40 minutes | Serves 8**

3.5 kg pork ribs - bone in and/or boneless, trimmed of excess fat
10 g black pepper
10 g onion powder
6 g garlic powder
2 g paprika (optional)

1. Mix pepper, onion powder, garlic powder, paprika, and salt in a bowl then rub over the ribs. Make sure all sides are covered.
2. Place the ribs into your air fryer breast side down and cook for 40 minutes until tender. Flip the ribs halfway through cooking them to ensure even browning.
3. Remove the ribs from the air fryer and serve!

## Air Fryer Catfish

**Prep Time: 5 minutes | Cook Time: 10 minutes | Serves 5**

5x200 g catfish fillets
3 g paprika
5 g salt
9 g pepper (black and/or white)
8.5 g onion powder

1. Mix the paprika, salt, pepper, and onion powder in a bowl then rub it all over the catfish fillets. Make sure to get all sides of the fish.
2. Place the fish into your air fryer and cook for 10 minutes until done.
3. Remove the fish from the air fryer and serve!

## Air Fryer Steak Bites and Mushrooms

**Prep Time: 5 minutes | Cook Time: 15 minutes | Serves 7-10**

500 g steak
100 g mushrooms, sliced
1 onion, diced
10 ml olive oil
8.5 g salt
2 g pepper
5 g garlic powder
30 ml Worcestershire Sauce

1. Preheat your air fryer to 180ºC.
2. In a bowl, mix the olive oil, salt, pepper, garlic powder, onion powder and Worcestershire Sauce then rub it all over the steak and mushroom slices. Make sure to get all sides of the food exposed to the spices.
3. Place mushrooms and steak into the air fryer breast side down then cook for 15 minutes until done or until they reach 80ºC at their thickest point.
4. Serve!

# Air Fryer Ginger Lime Prawns

**Prep Time: 5 minutes | Cook Time: 10 minutes | Serves 6**

500 g prawns, cleaned and deveined
30 ml lime juice
5 ml olive oil
3.5 g salt
3 g ginger powder
4.5 g pepper (black or white)
2 g garlic powder
3.5 g onion powder

1. Place the prawns into the air fryer in a single layer.
2. In a small bowl, mix the olive oil, lime juice, ginger, salt, pepper, garlic powder, and onion powder then rub it all over the prawns. Make sure to get all sides of the food exposed to the spices.
3. Cook prawns for 10 minutes flipping halfway through cooking and make sure they reach 75ºC at their thickest part or until they are fully cooked through completely.
4. Serve and enjoy!

# Air Fryer Tofu with Honey Garlic Sauce

**Prep Time: 5 minutes | Cook Time: 15 minutes | Serves 4**

500 g tofu, cut into cubes
2.5 g onion powder
2.5 g garlic powder
2.5 g honey
3.5 g lime zest (optional)

1. Place the tofu into your air fryer in a single layer and cook for 15 minutes or until 75ºC at its thickest part or until it is fully cooked through completely, flip halfway through cooking them to ensure even browning.
2. Using a whisk or hand mixer, mix the honey, lime zest (if using), garlic powder and onion powder in a small bowl.
3. Transfer cooked tofu to a smaller container then pour the honey garlic sauce over tofu and stir to coat all sides of it. Make sure each piece is coated evenly.
4. Serve once sauce has been absorbed into the tofu or drizzled over the top.

# Air Fryer Tuna Carbonara

**Prep Time: 5 minutes | Cook Time: 10 minutes | Serves 2**

2x150 g tuna steaks (or any fillets, boneless and skinless)
3.5 g paprika
3.5 g pepper
3.5 g onion powder
5.5 g garlic powder

1. Mix the paprika, pepper, onion powder, and garlic powder in a small bowl. Make sure to mix it well.
2. Line the tuna steaks in a single layer with the spice mixture then cook for 8-10 minutes flipping halfway through cooking.
3. Cook until the tuna is done or until it reaches 60ºC at its thickest point.
4. Serve and enjoy!

# Air fryer Chicken Tikka Kebab

**Prep Time: 5 minutes | Cook Time: 15 minutes | Serves 5**

500 g chicken breast, cut into cubes
20 ml olive oil
4.5 g onion powder
1.5 g garlic powder
5.5 g salt
2 g pepper
2 g turmeric powder

1. Place the chicken breast into your air fryer in a single layer and cook for 10 minutes or until 75ºC or until until completely cooked through, flip halfway through cooking to ensure even browning.
2. In a bowl, mix the salt, pepper, onion powder (if using), garlic powder and turmeric powder together then rub it all over the chicken. Make sure to get all sides of the food exposed to the spices.
3. Place the chicken into your air fryer in a single layer once more and cook for another 5 minutes until done or until 70ºC at its thickest part (internal temperature). Flip halfway through cooking to ensure even browning.
4. Serve and enjoy!

# Air fryer scallops

**Prep Time: 5 minutes | Cook Time: 8 minutes | Serves 2**

500 g scallops, cleaned and boneless, patted dry with a paper towel
5.5 g salt
2.5 g pepper (black or white)
5.5 g onion powder

1. Place the scallops into the air fryer in a single layer and cook for 8 minutes, flip halfway through cooking to ensure even browning.
2. Serve and enjoy!

# Air Fryer Sous Vide Chicken

**Prep Time: 15 minutes + marinade time | Cook Time: 15 minutes | Serves 4**

1 kg whole chicken, cleaned, skinless and boneless
30 ml olive oil
3.5 g salt
2 g pepper
2 g garlic powder
1 g onion powder

1. In a bowl, mix the olive oil, salt, pepper, garlic powder, and onion powder together then rub it all over the chicken. Make sure to get all sides of the food exposed to the spices. Marinate for at least one hour before cooking or overnight for a better flavour result (recommended).
2. Place the chicken in the air fryer in a single layer and cook for 15 minutes or until 75ºC at its thickest part or until completely cooked through, flip halfway through cooking to ensure even browning.
3. Serve and enjoy!

# Air fryer duck breast

**Prep Time: 5 minutes | Cook Time: 10 minutes | Serves 4**

500 g duck breast, cleaned and deboned, cut into small pieces
3 g salt
3.5 g pepper (black or white)
5.5 g garlic powder

1. Place the duck breast into the air fryer in a single layer and cook for 10 minutes or until 75ºC at its thickest part or until completely cooked through, flip halfway through cooking to ensure even browning.
2. Serve and enjoy!

# Air fryer chicken katsu

**Prep Time: 5 minutes | Cook Time: 2 minutes | Serves 3**

500 g chicken thighs, deboned and cut into small pieces
3.5 g salt
2 g pepper
2.5 g garlic powder
1 g onion powder
60 g cornstarch
2 eggs, whisked
60 ml avocado oil

1. In a bowl, mix the salt, pepper and onion powder together then rub it all over the chicken. Make sure to get all sides of the food exposed to the spices.
2. In a bowl, mix the cornstarch and eggs together then coat each piece of chicken in this mixture before frying in avocado oil until cooked through (about 1-2 minutes). If you don't have an immersion blender, just finely chop all of the ingredients before applying them onto each piece of chicken.
3. Serve with cooked rice and enjoy!

## Air Fryer Country Fried Steak

**Prep Time: 10 minutes | Cook Time: 15 minutes | Serves 4-5**

500 g country fried steak, cut into small pieces
2 g garlic powder
3.5 g salt
2 g pepper (black or white)
1 g onion powder

1. Place the steak into the air fryer in a single layer and cook for 10-15 minutes or until 75ºC at its thickest part or until completely cooked through, flip halfway through cooking to ensure even browning.
2. Serve and enjoy!

## Air fryer potato wedges

**Prep Time: 10 minutes | Cook Time: 15 minutes | Serves 5-6 wedges**

3x150 g medium-sized potatoes, peeled and cubed into small pieces
3 g salt
2 g black pepper
0.5 g parsley flakes
3.5 g garlic powder
7.5 ml olive oil
2.5 g onion powder
2 g oregano

1. Preheat air fryer to 200ºC.
2. In a bowl, mix the salt and pepper together then rub it over each piece of potato before placing it in the air fryer for 15 minutes or until cooked through and browned to your liking. Flip halfway through cooking to ensure even browning.
3. When your potatoes are cooked, place them on a plate and sprinkle with the parsley flakes and oregano before drizzling olive oil over them.

## Air Fryer Bacon-Wrapped Pork Tenderloin

**Prep Time: 10 minutes | Cook Time: 17 minutes | Serves 4-5**

500 g pork tenderloin, deboned, cut into small pieces
6.5 g salt
3.5 g black pepper
230 g bacon
5.5 g garlic powder
2 g onion powder
2.5 g paprika
3 g dried oregano

1. Preheat air fryer to 185ºC.
2. In a bowl, mix the salt and pepper together then coat each piece of pork in it before wrapping it in bacon (you want to use as much bacon as possible). Make sure to press down the bacon around the pork so it stays on while cooking.
3. Place all of these into your air fryer for 15 minutes or until 75ºC at its thickest part or until completely cooked through, flip halfway through cooking to ensure even browning.
4. In a bowl, mix the paprika, oregano and onion powder together then coat each piece of pork in this mixture before frying in avocado oil until cooked through (about 1-2 minutes). If you don't have an immersion blender, just finely chop all of the ingredients before applying them onto each piece of pork. Serve and enjoy!

## Air Fryer Jicama Fries Recipe (Chili Cheese Fries)

**Prep Time: 5 minutes | Cook Time: 8 minutes | Serves 2**

250 g large jicama root, peeled and cut into long strips like french fries
1.5 g salt
3 g black pepper
2.5 g chili powder
2.5 g paprika powder
1.5g cumin powder
20 ml soy sauce

1. Place all of the ingredients into a bowl. Mix it together well then transfer the mixture into a Ziploc bag or another container.
2. Put the bag into the air fryer and cook for 8 minutes on 200ºC (for medium crispiness). Turn off the heat before 10 minutes are up.
3. Now, serve fresh or prepared according to your personal preference.

# Air Fried Cauliflower Wings

**Prep Time: 12 minutes | Cook Time: 35 minutes | Serves 2**

120 g cauliflower head, cut into small florets (stems may be left whole)
3 g salt
2.5 g black pepper
7 g paprika powder
2 g cayenne pepper
2.5 g parsley flakes
80 g ground chicken or turkey (optional)
3g garlic powder
1.5 g onion powder
1 g oregano

1. Preheat the air fryer to 200ºC for 2 minutes. Place the bell pepper, broccoli, cauliflower, and green onion in the 200ºC preheated air fryer for 15 minutes.
2. Set your oven to 200ºC post-production for 5 minutes (use temperature dial). Meanwhile, mix the ground turkey or chicken with the paprika powder, cumin powder, oregano, and black pepper.
3. Fluff the cauliflower florets in a bowl with a fork then place them in the preheated oven for 5 minutes (watch carefully!). Remove from the oven and set aside.
4. Take the cauliflower florets out of the oven and set aside. Meanwhile, mix the parsley flakes with 1.5g of salt to prepare a marinade for the chicken or turkey.
5. Add the garlic powder, onion powder, cayenne pepper, and paprika powder to the mixture you prepared for the chicken or turkey. Place the cauliflower florets in a bowl and add the marinade. Mix well so that all of the florets are coated.
6. Add the prepared cauliflower florets to the oven and cook for 2-3 minutes. Remove from heat and arrange on a plate ready to be served. Brush the chicken or turkey with the marinade and place it inside the preheated air fryer. Cook for 5 minutes, or until done.

# Air Fryer Crispy Chicken Tenders

**Prep Time: 15 minutes | Cook time: 5 minutes | Serves 2**

2x200 g chicken cutlets, cut in strips
150 g cream cheese, softened
3 g garlic, minced
2 g parsley flakes
1.5 g salt
1.5 g cayenne pepper
1.5 g paprika powder
2.5 g black pepper

1. Mix cream cheese, garlic and cayenne pepper in a bowl until they are well combined.
2. Place the chicken strips into a bowl and pour over the cream cheese mixture. Mix well so that all of the chicken strips are coated.
3. Add in salt, paprika and black pepper to the chicken strips and mix again so that all of them are coated.
4. Transfer into the preheated air fryer and cook for 5 minutes at 200ºC.
5. Take the chicken out of the heat and give it a final mix so that all of the pieces are better distributed in the air fryer.
6. Serve immediately.

## Air Fryer Bacon Avocado Fries

**Prep Time: 5 minutes | Cook Time: 5 minutes | Serve 4**

4 sliced avocados, slice the avocado so that it is as thick as a french fry
4 rashers, thinly sliced bacon
60 ml Ranch Sauce
6 g salt
3 g pepper

1. Preheat the air fryer to 200ºC for 2 minutes and then remove the avocado from the freezer. Transfer them into the preheated air fryer for 4 minutes until they are warm.
2. Fold in your ranch sauce and bacon and season with salt and pepper to taste.
3. Serve immediately with a nice selection of your favorite condiments.

## Air Fryer Butterflied Lemon Chicken

**Prep Time: 10 minutes | Cook time: 15 minutes | Serves 3**

4 chicken breasts, (250-300g)
2 eggs
2.5 g salt (optional)
15 ml soy sauce
2 g cayenne pepper
1.5 g black pepper, ground
1.5 g garlic powder
1 g chili flakes (optional)
1 g cumin powder
2 Lemons (sliced into 8 wedges)

1. Preheat the air fryer to 200ºC for 2 minutes.
2. Butterfly the chicken breasts by slicing them down the middle and open them up with your hands, flat like a book. Season with salt, black pepper and cayenne pepper.
3. Transfer the opened chicken breasts to the preheated air fryer and cook for 10 minutes at 200ºC.
4. Meanwhile, beat the eggs in a bowl with 1g of salt. Pour into the same bowl and mix well so that all of the egg is beaten.
5. Add the soy sauce and mix again so that all of the egg is well-combined with soy sauce.
6. Take the chicken out of the air fryer and top with the egg mixture. Then transfer the chicken breasts back in for 5 more minutes.
7. Remove from heat and serve immediately with lemon wedges.

# Air Fryer Arancini (Rice Balls)

**Prep time: 10 minutes | Cook time: 15 minutes | Serves 10**

400 g cooked rice
15 g All-purpose flour
1 egg
1 g salt
1.5 g black pepper, ground
15 g Parmesan cheese
30 ml oil (optional)

1. Mix the rice, parmesan cheese, salt and pepper together in a bowl then form balls about the size of a ping-pong ball with your hands.
2. Place them on a plate, cover with plastic wrap and refrigerate for 30 minutes
3. Remove the plastic wrap and beat the egg in a bowl. Dip each of the balls into the egg one at a time then coat them with flour.
4. Transfer to the plate and place it in the freezer for 30 minutes.
5. Heat up 30ml of oil in a large saucepan over medium-high heat. Brown each rice ball on every side and transfer them into the air fryer for 15 minutes at 200ºC.
6. Serve warm with your favorite dipping sauce.

# Air Fryer Turkey Croquettes

**Prep time: 10 minutes | Cook time: 20 minutes | Serves 8-10**

2.5 g salt
8-10 turkey breast fillets, shredded
15 ml oil (optional)
50 ml water
15 ml Worcestershire sauce (optional) (Note: can substitute with tomato sauce)
1.5 g garlic powder
1 g black pepper, ground
2 g cayenne pepper

1. Shred the turkey into small pieces, about the size of a walnut. If the meat if very tender, you can use a knife to chop it up but in most cases, you'll need to shred it with your hands
2. Heat oil in a large skillet over medium heat. Add the garlic powder, black pepper and cayenne pepper then stir well.
3. Add the turkey to the pan and fry for 4-5 minutes until it is browned then add salt and water. Stir well, until all of the water has evaporated
4. Add the Worcestershire sauce and keep stirring until everything is well combined.
5. Transfer the mixture into the air fryer for 10-15 minutes at 200ºC or until it is completely cooked.

# Air fryer sticky pork belly bites

**Prep time: 10 minutes | Cook time: 10 minutes | Serves 6-8**

80 g pork belly, diced (Note: If you are using a leaner cut of pork, add 15ml of oil to the meat)
1.5 g salt
15 ml ketchup
15 ml Worcestershire sauce (optional) (Note: you can replace this with tomato sauce)
1.5 g garlic powder
1 g black pepper, ground
2 g cayenne pepper
1.5 g onion powder
1 g sugar (optional)

1. Heat oil in a large saucepan over high heat until the oil is hot to touch and shimmering. Add the pork belly and cook until both sides are browned.
2. Add the onion powder, garlic powder, cayenne pepper and sugar to the pan then stir well. Add salt and Worcestershire sauce (or tomato sauce) to taste.
3. Stir until all of the water has evaporated and then transfer the mixture into the air fryer for 8-10 minutes at 200°C.

Remove from heat and serve warm.

# Air Fryer Fish And Sweet Potato Chips

**Prep time: 10 minutes | Cook time: 10 minutes | Serves 2**

400 g sweet potato, peeled, cut into fries
360 g white fish fillets, cut into portions
1 egg
1 g salt
1.5 g black pepper, ground
30 ml oil (optional)

1. Preheat the air fryer to 200°C for 2-3 minutes then remove the fish and potato from the freezer. Transfer into the preheated air fryer for 4-5 minutes until it is warm.
2. Massage the potato and fish with some of the egg to create a crispy coating. Place them on a plate then brush with oil and season with salt and pepper to taste.
3. Bake them in the preheated air fryer for 10-12 minutes at 200°C. Serve immediately with your favorite sauce.

## Air Fryer Fish Tacos

**Prep time: 20 minutes | Cook time: 25 minutes | Serves 2-4**

1 red onion, sliced into thin strips
15 ml oil (optional)
120 g tilapia fillet, cut into medium sized pieces (you can also use other types of fish)
1.5 g salt
1 g black pepper, ground
2 g cayenne pepper
2.5 g garlic powder
1.5 g onion powder
30 ml lemon juice (fresh if possible) (Note: you can substitute with lime juice or a combination of both)

1. Heat up the air fryer to 200ºC for 2-3 minutes then remove the fish. Add oil to a large saucepan and heat it until the oil is hot to touch and shimmering. Add the onion and cook over high heat until it is browned and softens. Add the garlic powder, cayenne pepper and spices then stir well to combine.
2. Add the fish to the pan, lemon juice and water (or lime) and cook for 10 minutes over medium heat until it is fully cooked then transfer into the air fryer for 10-15 minutes at 200ºC.
3. Serve warm with tortilla chips or hard shell tacos.

## Air Fryer Spinach And Feta Quiche

**Prep time: 15 minutes | Cook time: 15 minutes | Serves 4**

200 g frozen spinach, defrosted and squeezed dry (Note: you can use fresh spinach. Just add it to the food processor and pulse a few times until it reaches a puree)
2.5 g salt
15 ml olive oil (optional)
1.5 g black pepper, ground
360 g feta, crumbled (Note: You can replace this with other types of cheese such as cheddar cheese)
4 eggs, lightly beaten

1. Preheat the air fryer to 200ºC for 2-3 minutes then remove the dough from the freezer. Spread the dough over the bottom of the air fryer basket and let it cook for 10 minutes.
2. Transfer into the preheated air fryer and add all of the ingredients except for the feta cheese. Stir well then transfer into the air fryer and cook for 12-15 minutes at 200ºC.
3. Remove from heat, top with feta cheese, slice it up and serve warm with your favorite salad or a side of chips.

# CHAPTER 4: SNACK RECIPES

## Air Fryer Spiced Chickpeas

**Prep Time: 5 minutes | Cook Time: 20 minutes | Serves 4**

340 g chickpeas
4 g ground cumin
2 g chilli powder
2 g cayenne pepper
1.5 g ground black pepper
3.5 g salt
60 ml olive oil
4 g lemon zest

1. Turn on the air fryer to 250°C and while it is heating up, rinse and drain the chickpeas.
2. Mix all spices together in a bowl, add olive oil and mix until smooth.
3. Add chickpeas, mix until evenly coated, then spread on a tray with parchment paper so they are in one layer.
4. Bake for 10 minutes, then roll them around and bake for another 10 to make sure they are cooked. Cool.
5. Transfer to an airtight container and store in a cool place. Serve and enjoy with your favourite dish.

## Air Fryer Baked Oatmeal

**Prep Time: 5 minutes | Cook Time: 25 minutes | Serves 4**

340 g rolled oats, quick cooking
3 g ground cumin
2.5 g chilli powder
4 g cayenne pepper
1.5 g ground black pepper
3 g salt
60 ml olive oil

1. Preheat the air fryer to 270°C and while it is heating up, mix oats, ground spices and salt in a bowl, add olive oil and mix until evenly coated.
2. Spread oats in one layer using parchment paper, then bake for 15 minutes, then roll them around and bake for another 10 minutes to make sure they are cooked.
3. Cool and store in an airtight container.
4. Serve and enjoy.

## Air Fryer Courgette Chips

**Prep Time: 5 minutes | Cook Time: 30 minutes | Serves 4**

340 g courgette (cleaned, sliced into strips and dried)
5 g ground cumin
3 g chilli powder
2.5 g cayenne pepper
2 g ground black pepper
2.5 g salt
65 ml olive oil (for oilier chips use more)

1. Turn on the air fryer to 250°C and while it is heating up, drizzle the courgette with olive oil to help it cook evenly. Mix all spices together in a bowl.
2. Add courgette and mix until evenly coated, then spread on a tray with parchment paper so they are in one layer.
3. Bake for 20 minutes, then roll them around and bake for another 10 minutes until golden brown.
4. Cool and store in an airtight container.
5. Serve and enjoy.

## Air Fryer Potato Chips

**Prep Time: 5 minutes | Cook Time: 25 minutes | Serves 4**

340 g potato slices
5 g ground cumin
3 g chilli powder
2 g cayenne pepper
1.5 g ground black pepper
5 g salt
70 ml olive oil

1. Preheat the air fryer to 250°C.
2. Mix all spices together in a bowl, add olive oil and mix until smooth.
3. Add potatoes, mix well to evenly coat them, then spread on a tray with parchment paper so they are in one layer.
4. Bake for 15 minutes, then roll them around and bake for another 10 to make sure they are cooked. Cook until golden brown.
5. Transfer to an airtight container and store in a cool place.
6. Serve and enjoy

# Air Fryer Sugary Pecans

**Prep Time: 5 minutes | Cook Time: 30 minutes | Serves 8**

2 g cinnamon
1 g nutmeg
6 g salt
400 ml water
4 ml vanilla extract
300 g pecan nougat
28 g salted butter, melted
2 egg whites

1. Turn on the air fryer to 200°C and while it is heating up, mix all ingredients in a bowl besides melted butter, until water is well incorporated.
2. Pour melted butter in a separate bowl.
3. Add egg white in the other bowl then add pecan mixture to it and stir well until they are evenly incorporated.
4. Spread on a baking tray with parchment paper then put in the air fryer. Bake for 30 minutes.
5. Remove from the oven and let cool on a cooling rack while you put the rest of it in a container or baggy and store in the fridge or freezer until ready to use.

# Air Fryer Baba Ganoush

**Prep Time: 5 minutes | Cook Time: 20 minutes | Serves 4**

320 g eggplant
2 g garlic powder
3 g zatar
4 g onion powder
20 ml olive oil
3 ml lemon juice

1. Chop eggplants into small pieces and put into a bowl with all ingredients except the olive oil.
2. Put the bowl into the air fryer and bake for 10 minutes then roll them around and bake for another 10 to make sure it is cooked.
3. Transfer to a colander/strainer and let cool.
4. In small batches, put into food processor and blend until smooth
5. Add olive oil to the mixture then transfer to an airtight container or baggy, store in the fridge or freezer until ready to use.

## Air Fryer Hot Pickle Chips

**Prep Time: 5 minutes | Cook Time: 20 minutes | Serves 4**

190 g pickle
2 g salt
4 g garlic powder
40 ml olive oil
2.5 ml lemon juice

1. Chop pickle into small pieces and put into a bowl with all ingredients except olive oil.
2. Put the bowl into the air fryer and bake for 10 minutes then roll them around and bake for another 10 to make sure it is cooked. Transfer to a strainer, let cool.
3. In small batches, put into food processor and blend until smooth.
4. Add olive oil to the mixture then transfer to an airtight container or baggy, store in the fridge or freezer until ready to use.

## Air Fryer Ham And Cheese Crescent Rolls

**Prep Time: 5 minutes | Cook Time: 20 minutes | Serves 8**

30 g baking powder
1 g salt
85 ml water
65 g cheese
100 g ham

1. Mix all ingredients together in a bowl until dough is smooth, then roll into 4 balls, cover with plastic wrap and let rest for 15 minutes
2. Roll dough into a rectangle about 0.5cm thick and cut it into 8 pieces
3. Put one piece at a time in between two pieces of parchment paper then roll out to 3x its size to form a crescent shape
4. Bake for 10 minutes then flip over and bake for another 10 to make sure it is cooked.
5. Remove from the oven and let cool on a cooling rack while you put the rest of it in a container or baggy and store in the fridge or freezer until ready to use.

# Air Fryer Steak Jerky

**Prep Time: 5 minutes | Cook Time: 20 minutes | Serves 4**

300 g beef steaks
2 g garlic powder
250 ml soy sauce
1.5 g chilli pepper flakes (optional)
300 g brown sugar
3 ml lemon juice

1. Chop steak into small pieces and put into a bowl with all ingredients except soy sauce, brown sugar and lemon juice.
2. Put the bowl into the air fryer and bake for 10 minutes then roll them around and bake for another 10 to make sure it is cooked.
3. Transfer to a colander/strainer, let cool.
4. In small batches, put into food processor and blend until smooth.
5. Add soy sauce, brown sugar and lemon juice then transfer to an airtight container or baggy, store in the fridge or freezer until ready to use.

# Air Fryer Sweet Wontons

**Prep Time: 5 minutes | Cook Time: 20 minutes | Serves 4**

250 g wontons
2.5 g salt
170 g brown sugar
20 ml olive oil
90 g blueberries

1. Hand mix all ingredients in a bowl then put wontons on a baking tray with parchment paper then put in the air fryer.
2. Bake for 10 minutes then flip and bake for another 10 to make sure it is cooked.
3. Transfer to a colander/strainer, let cool.
4. In small batches, put into food processor and blend until smooth.
5. Add olive oil to the mixture then transfer to an airtight container or baggy, store in the fridge or freezer until ready to use.

## Air Fryer Cottage Fries

**Prep Time: 10 minutes | Cook Time: 15 minutes | Serves 4**

450g sweet potatoes, peeled and cut into 2cm cubes
15ml olive oil
2g fresh rosemary, finely chopped
2g fresh thyme, finely chopped
6g salt
3g black pepper

1. Preheat the air fryer to 180ºC
2. In a large bowl, mix together the sweet potatoes with 2g each of rosemary and thyme and 3g of salt and pepper until coated.
3. Pour about a third of the sweet potatoes into a skillet sprayed lightly with olive oil cooking spray and cook for 5 minutes or until tender.
4. Transfer them to a paper towel-lined plate, and repeat with the remaining sweet potatoes; once cooled, return them to the large bowl.
5. Place the skillet back over medium heat and spray with olive oil cooking spray. Return the potatoes to the pan and toss well until evenly coated in oil.
6. Pour them onto a paper towel-lined plate; repeat with the remaining sweet potatoes.
7. Place a cooling rack over a baking sheet and place on top of the air fryer, cook for 10 minutes or until golden brown
8. Serve and enjoy.

## Air Fryer Hush Puppies

**Prep Time: 5 minutes | Cook Time: 30 minutes | Serves 4**

100 g yellow cornmeal
55 g baking flour
1 g baking powder
170 ml milk
240 ml oil
2 g salt
2 g black pepper
1 egg
1.5 g paprika
240 ml water

1. Mix all ingredients except oil, water and egg then add the oil and water while mixing to make dough then put aside for 5 minutes.
2. Bake for 10 minutes then roll them around and bake for another 10 to make sure it is cooked.
3. Toss in an air fryer for 10 minutes until cooked.
4. Drain excess oil and transfer to a colander/strainer, let cool
5. Put into food processor and blend until smooth
6. Add olive oil to the mixture then transfer to an airtight container or baggy, store in the fridge or freezer until ready to use.

## Air Fryer Buffalo Cauliflower Bites

**Prep Time: 5 minutes | Cook Time: 60 minutes | Serves 6**

| | |
|---|---|
| 500 g cauliflower florets | 180 ml buffalo sauce |
| 2.5 g salt | 1 egg white |

1. Mix all ingredients except egg white and buffalo sauce in a bowl then transfer to an air fryer.
2. Bake for 15 minutes then roll them around and bake for another 20 to make sure it is cooked.
3. Put the egg white in a bowl, beat them then roll the cauliflower bits in it until well coated
4. Put into an air fryer and bake again for 25 minutes until cooked through
5. Transfer to a colander/strainer, let cool.
6. In small batches put into food processor and blend until smooth
7. Add buffalo sauce to the mixture then transfer to an airtight container or baggy, store in the fridge or freezer until ready to use.

## Air Fryer Mozzarella Sticks with Marinara & Sun-Dried Tomato

**Prep Time: 5 minutes | Cook Time: 15 minutes | Serves 4**

| | |
|---|---|
| 270 g mozzarella (shredded) | 120 ml tomato sauce |
| 95 g sun-dried tomatoes (crushed) | 280 ml olive oil |
| | 120 g chives (finely sliced) |

1. In a frying pan, add tomato paste and olive oil then cook until paste is slightly brown.
2. Mix all ingredients except chives in a bowl (mozzarella, tomato paste, olive oil, sun-dried tomatoes and chives).
3. Bake for 15 minutes or until well cooked.
4. Mix chives in with mixture in a food processor until smooth then transfer to an airtight container or baggy, store in the fridge or freezer until ready to use.

## Air Fryer Toasted Ravioli

**Prep Time: 5 minutes | Cook Time: 10 minutes | Serves 2**

5 g butter
2 g parsley
1.5 g garlic powder
2 egg whites
1.5 g salt
300 g flour
1.5 g paprika

1. In a frying pan, add butter and cook until light brown (do not let it burn). Add parsley and garlic powder then cook for a further 20 seconds. Set aside to cool.
2. In a bowl, mix all ingredients for the dough until well combined then transfer to an air fryer pan.
3. Bake for 10-12 minutes or until well cooked.
4. Transfer to a colander/strainer, let cool.
5. In small batches, put into food processor and blend until smooth.
6. Transfer to an airtight container or baggy, store in the fridge or freezer until ready to use.

## Air Fryer Spanakopita Bites

**Prep Time: 5 minutes | Cook time: 20 minutes | Serves 3**

250 g feta (crumbled)
250 g spinach (roughly chopped)
5 ml lemon juice
1 egg white
100 ml olive oil
2 g cinnamon powder

1. Mix all ingredients except for the spinach and feta in a bowl then transfer to an air fryer.
2. Blend spinach and feta for around 20 seconds in a food processor then add to the mixture.
3. Fill in an air fryer pan with olive oil then cook for 20 minutes or until well cooked.
4. Transfer to a colander, let cool.
5. In small batches, put into food processor and blend until smooth.
6. Add spinach and feta mixture to the mixture then transfer to an airtight container or baggy, store in the fridge or freezer until ready to use.

## Air Fryer Nachos

**Prep Time: 5 minutes | Cook time: 15 minutes | Serves 2**

200 g tortilla chips (preferably homemade
120 g cheese (shredded)
5 g salt
80 g black olives (sliced)

1. Heat up a pan and add chips and olive oil
2. Cook for 30 seconds or until lightly browned then remove from the pan and set aside to cool.
3. in a bowl, mix all ingredients except the nachos (nacho cheese, tortilla chips and olives) until well combined.
4. Transfer to an air fryer then bake for 15 minutes or until cooked through.
5. Transfer to a colander, let cool.
6. In small batches put into food processor and blend until smooth.
7. Add nacho cheese and tortilla chips to the mixture then transfer to an airtight container or baggy, store in the fridge or freezer until ready to use.

## Air Fryer Chicken and Hummus Stew

**Prep Time: 5 minutes | Cook time: 10 minutes | Serves 3**

4 chicken thigh slices (diced)
250 g cucumber (sliced)
100 g garlic
20 g parsley leaves (sliced)
5 g salt
2.5 g all spice
3.5 g ground coriander
10 g sesame seeds
50 ml olive oil
200 ml water

1. Add seasoning mixes to the onion (excluding the olive oil).
2. Season the chicken with salt/pepper, sesame seeds, coriander and all spice then place in an air fryer pan. Cook for 10 minutes or until cooked through. Transfer to a colander, let cool.
3. In small batches put into food processor and blend until smooth.
4. Add cucumber and garlic then transfer to an airtight container or baggy, store in the fridge until ready to use.

## Air Fryer Cheese Breadsticks

**Prep Time: 5 minutes | Cook time: 12 minutes | Serves 3**

150 g cheese
1 egg white
50 g flour
3 g salt
60 ml olive oil
1.5 g paprika

1. In a bowl, mix all ingredients apart from the cheese and flour then place in an air fryer pan.
2. In a bowl, add salt, paprika and olive oil to onion then mix well then transfer to an air fryer pan.
3. Bake for 12 minutes or until cooked through. Transfer to a colander, let cool.
4. In small batches, put into food processor and blend until smooth.
5. Add cheese and flour to the mixture then transfer to an airtight container or baggy, store in the fridge or freezer until ready to use.

## Air Fryer Baked Onion Rings

**Prep Time: 5 minutes | Cook Time: 12 minutes | Serves 2**

200 g onion
40 ml olive oil
1.5 g garlic powder
1.5 g salt
20 g baking flour
150 g cheese (shredded)

1. Preheat an air fryer to 160ºC then in a bowl, mix all ingredients apart from the cheese and flour then place in an air fryer.
2. In a bowl, add salt, garlic powder and olive oil to onion and mix well then transfer to an air fryer pan.
3. Bake for 12 minutes or until well cooked through.
4. Transfer to a colander, let cool in small batches, put into food processor and blend until smooth.
5. Transfer to an airtight container or baggy, store in the fridge or freezer until ready to use.

# CHAPTER 5: DESSERT RECIPES

# Air Fryer Lava Cakes

**Prep Time: 10 minutes | Cook Time: 15 minutes | Serves 2**

80 g semi-sweet chocolate chips
55 g butter
2 eggs
5 ml vanilla extract
1.5 g salt
25 g all-purpose flour
55 g powdered sugar
30 g Nutella

1. Preheat your air fryer to 185ºC.
2. In a medium microwave-safe bowl, add the chocolate chips and butter and heat on 30-second increments until completely melted and smooth, stirring during each interval.
3. Add the eggs, vanilla, salt, flour, and powdered sugar to the bowl and whisk to combine.
4. In a separate bowl, mix the Nutella, softened butter, and powdered sugar.
5. Prepare the ramekins by spraying them with oil and fill each one-half full with the chocolate chip mixture. Add half of the Nutella filling in the center of each ramekin, then top off with the remaining chocolate chip mixture making sure the Nutella is covered.
6. Carefully place the lava cakes into the air fryer and cook for 8 to 11 minutes.
7. Carefully remove the lava cakes from the air fryer and allow them to cool for 5 minutes. Take a butterknife and run around the outside edges of the cake and flip out onto a serving plate.
8. Top with ice cream, chocolate syrup and/or other toppings and enjoy!

# Air Fryer Baked Apples

**Prep Time: 5 minutes | Cook Time: 15 minutes | Serves 4**

4x200 g large apples
15 g quick oats
20 g golden raisins
13 g chopped pecans
25 g light brown sugar
15 ml melted unsalted butter
1.5 g apple pie seasoning

1. Cut the tops of your apples off to remove the stem. Then also slightly cut the bottom of your apple off so that it is flat on the bottom, so it does not roll in the air fryer.
2. Using an apple corer or a paring knife, remove the center of the apple, careful not to go all the way through the bottom. Then your filling will leak out as it cooks. I made the diameter of my cut-out about 2.5cm wide. You don't want to cut too much of the apple out, but you still want all that delicious filling in there.
3. In a medium bowl, combine the oats, raisins, pecans, brown sugar, melted butter, and apple pie seasoning.
4. Divide the mixture among the 4 apples, filling in the centers.
5. Place your apples in the air fryer and bake at 150ºC for 13-15 minutes, till they are your desired amount of softness.
6. Allow them to sit for a few minutes, as they will be very hot to remove. Once you have removed them, serve warm and for an additional treat, top with a dollop of vanilla ice cream.

# Air Fryer Chocolate Chip Biscuits

**Prep Time: 10 minutes | Cook Time: 8 minutes | Serves 7**

1.5 g baking soda
2 eggs, beaten with a fork to combine
5 ml vanilla extract (optional)
6 g brown sugar
25 g butter, melted
28 g granulated sugar
1.5 g kosher salt
225 g all-purpose flour
2 g cocoa powder

1. Preheat your air fryer to 150ºC and use a baking sheet on the rack below to prevent any spills when removing the biscuits from the air fryer. In a large bowl, combine the eggs and vanilla. This is optional, but it makes a better biscuit and makes them slightly chewy if you use it. This can be done in advance as well.
2. Add the sugars, melted butter, salt and flour to the egg mixture. Mix together and then add the cocoa powder.
3. Spoon 10g of dough each onto your baking sheet, or just enough to cover the bottom of the sheet. Press down on each biscuit with a fork in a criss-cross pattern to flatten it out a little bit and bake for 8 minutes, rotating the pan halfway through. Allow your biscuits to cool for 5 minutes on the pan before transferring them to a cooling rack or plate.
4. Enjoy!

# Air Fryer Carrot Cake

**Prep Time: 5 minutes | Cook Time: 15 minutes | Serves 12**

240 g carrots, grated
70 g butter, melted
220 g all-purpose flour
1.5 g baking powder
1 g salt
50 g sugar
1.5 g cinnamon
2 g nutmeg
2 eggs, lightly beaten
75 ml vegetable oil

1. Preheat the air fryer to 185ºC. Prepare the bread pan by spraying with nonstick spray and set aside. In a large bowl, mix all dry ingredients together, including grated carrots, mix well and set aside. In a medium bowl, add all wet ingredients and whisk together. Add dry ingredients to wet and mix until just combined (don't overmix).
2. Using an ice cream scoop or two spoons, pour batter into the bread pan and spread out a little bit.
3. Toast the bread for 12-15 minutes, or until bread is lightly browned in spots.
4. Serve with whipped cream if desired.

## Air Fryer Banana Bread

**Prep Time: 5 minutes | Cook Time: 40 minutes | Serves 12**

2 g baking powder
15 g all-purpose flour, sifted
1 banana, mashed with a fork
8.5 ml coconut oil
3 eggs, beaten with a fork
1.5 g salt
1 ml vanilla extract

1. Preheat your air fryer to 175ºC and prepare a bread pan by spraying it with nonstick spray. In a large bowl, mix the flour, baking powder, salt, and mashed banana together. In a medium bowl, combine the eggs and melted coconut oil together. Pour the wet ingredients into the dry ingredients and mix thoroughly (don't overmix). Add in 1ml vanilla extract and mix until combined.
2. Pour batter into the bread pan and bake at 175ºC for 40 minutes, or until cake springs back when touched in the center. Allow to cool for 5 minutes and remove from pan by flipping it upside down off of the pan. Place on a cooling rack to cool completely before slicing.

## Air Fryer Cinnamon Sugar Dessert Fries

**Prep Time: 2 minutes | Cook Time: 10 minutes | Serves 4**

1.5 g baking soda
400 g sweet potato, cut into wedges
30 ml canola oil
2.5 g cinnamon, divided
1.5 g salt

1. Preheat your air fryer to 190ºC and spray a glass baking dish with nonstick spray. In a small bowl, mix the baking soda and cinnamon. In a medium bowl, add all dry ingredients, mixing well. Add canola oil and mix until combined.
2. Dip each wedge of potatoes into the mixture, coating every corner and place them on your prepared baking dish.
3. Bake for 10 minutes, turning as needed until potatoes are golden brown in color. Allow to cool for 5 minutes and serve warm with a dollop of unsweetened vanilla ice cream, or another sauce of your choice!

# Air Fryer Pumpkin Pie Twists

**Prep Time: 5 minutes | Cook Time: 25 minutes | Serves 12**

220 g pumpkin puree (canned or prepared)
2 eggs, beaten with a fork
1.5 g baking powder
1 g baking soda
1.5 ml vanilla extract
45 g butter, melted and cooled to room temperature
30 ml pumpkin spice cooking wine (or apple cider)
7.5 g cinnamon, divided

1. In a medium bowl, combine all dry ingredients except for 1.5g cinnamon. Mix until well combined and set aside. In a large bowl, mix all wet ingredients together. Add the dry ingredients to the wet, mixing until just combined (don't overmix).
2. Use a biscuit scoop or spoon to scoop dough onto your air fryer baking pan or on a silicone mat in a baking dish. Press each dough ball into a flat circle and place into the air fryer on either the top rack or bottom rack (depending on how many you are making).
3. Bake for 10 minutes, turn over and bake an additional 10-15 minutes until lightly browned and set. Allow to cool completely before serving.

# Air Fryer Pineapple Upside-Down Cake

**Prep Time: 5 minutes | Cook Time: 25 minutes | Serves 8-10**

1 g baking powder
8 eggs, separated
240 ml pineapple juice
8.5 g brown sugar, packed
120 g butter, melted and cooled
180 g flour, sifted
1.5 g baking soda
1.5 g salt

1. Preheat your air fryer to 175ºC and spray a bread pan with nonstick spray. In a large bowl, beat egg whites and set aside.
2. In a medium bowl, add all other ingredients except for the egg whites and whisk until well combined.
3. Add wet ingredients to the egg whites, mixing on low speed until just combined but don't over mix (just until it looks uniform).
4. Pour batter into the bread pan and bake for 25 minutes, or until a toothpick inserted in the center comes out clean.
5. Allow to cool for 5 minutes, then remove from pan by flipping it upside down off of the pan.
6. Place on a cooling rack and allow to completely cool before serving.

# Air Fryer Strawberry Nutella Hand Pies

**Prep Time: 10 minutes | Cook Time: 25 minutes | Serves 4-6**

130 g Nutella
112 g strawberry jam
1.5 ml strawberry extract
180 g flour, sifted
2.5 g baking powder
130 ml buttermilk,
room temperature
1 ml vanilla extract
1 egg, beaten with a fork
45 ml melted butter, cooled
2.5 g cinnamon, divided

1. Preheat your air fryer to 175ºC and spray a glass baking dish with nonstick spray. In a medium bowl, mix all dry ingredients together.
2. In a small bowl, mix all wet ingredients together (except for the melted butter). Pour wet into dry and stir until just combined (do not overmix). Pour into the glass baking pan and spread out a little bit.
3. Bake for 25 minutes, or until set. Allow to completely cool on a cooling rack. When completely cooled, cut into triangles and place on a baking tray lined with parchment paper and allow to cool completely before filling between the wedges.
4. To make the filling, combine all ingredients aside from the melted butter (but not cooled). Pour the liquefied mixture over the hand pie wedges and top with a dollop of melted butter.

# Air Fryer Peanut Butter Banana Energy Bites

**Prep Time: 10 minutes | Cook Time: 15 minutes | Serves 12**

25 g peanut butter
275 g bananas, sliced
3 ml vanilla extract
0.5 g baking soda
2.5 g baking powder
90 ml buttermilk,
room temperature

1. Grease a biscuit sheet and preheat your air fryer to 175ºC. In a medium bowl, mix all dry ingredients together (except baking soda). In a large bowl combine all wet ingredients (peanut butter and banana) until combined.
2. Add dry ingredients and mix until well combined. Lay out a few spoonfuls of the batter to cover your biscuit sheet.
3. Bake in the air fryer for 12-15 minutes, or until lightly browned (cooking time will vary), and allow to cool on a cooling rack.
4. While the bites are baking, place parchment paper on a biscuit sheet and place frozen bananas in between layers. When the bites have cooled, crumble them up into a food processor and pulse until smooth (it may take a few minutes). Slowly add your banana puree to the mashed bananas in between layers and smooth it out. Allow to freeze.

# Air Fryer Pumpkin Applesauce Muffins

**Prep Time: 10 minutes | Cook Time: 20 minutes | Serves 24**

120 g flour, sifted
3 g salt
100 g pumpkin puree
30 ml melted coconut oil, cooled
30 ml vanilla extract
90 ml buttermilk, room temperature
1.5 g baking powder
60 ml applesauce
100 ml canned pumpkin
120 ml water
1.5 g cinnamon, divided

1. Preheat your air fryer to 175ºC and spray your pan with nonstick spray. In a large bowl, whisk the flour, baking powder, and salt.
2. In a small bowl, combine cooled coconut oil, applesauce, vanilla extract, pumpkin puree and water together.
3. Add wet ingredients to dry and mix until just combined (do not over mix).
4. Spray your biscuit sheet with nonstick and spoon out heaping tablespoon of batter onto the pan. Top with an apple slice and sprinkle with cinnamon.
5. Bake for 17-20 minutes, or until a toothpick inserted in the center comes out clean. Cool on a cooling rack completely before serving.

# Air Fryer Twix Cheesecake

**Prep Time: 15 minutes | Cook Time: 20 minutes | Serves 8-10**

200 g Twix bars, crushed
140 g cream cheese, softened (room temperature)
1.5 ml vanilla extract
30 ml water
1 g sugar (to be added after baking)

1. Preheat your air fryer to 175ºC. In a small saucepan, add the cream cheese and vanilla extract and heat until all the ingredients are just combined together.
2. Prepare Twix and caramel sauce as per the instructions provided.
3. When Twix is completely cooled, add to cream cheese mixture and mix until just combined (do not over mix).
4. Pour into a baking dish with a spatula or spoon and top with caramel sauce. Bake for 15-20 minutes in your air fryer.
5. Allow to cool completely on a cooling rack before serving.

## Air Fryer Oreos

**Prep Time: 10 minutes | Cook Time: 15 minutes | Serves 9**

130 g oreo biscuits, crushed (18-20 depending on the size of your biscuit press)
30 ml melted butter, cooled (to be added during the last minute)
60 ml light cream (room temperature)

1. Mix all the ingredients together except for the cream and butter.
2. Place on a spoon and press biscuit into the air fryer for 12-15 minutes, or until lightly browned.
3. Take out at this time and use a heat resistant spatula to smooth out the bottom of the cheesecake if it has cracked.
4. Once cooled, drizzle the melted butter on top and cut into slices.

## Air Fryer Bananas Foster

**Prep Time: 10 minutes | Cook Time: 15 minutes | Serves 1**

80 g cinnamon and sugar, mixed
2 bananas, sliced in half long ways (preferably frozen)
2.5 ml vanilla extract
1.5 g baking powder (optional, but highly recommended)

1. Preheat your air fryer to 170ºC and spray your baking dish with nonstick spray. In a medium bowl, mix all dry ingredients together (minus the vanilla extract).
2. In a small bowl, add sliced bananas and sprinkle with cinnamon and sugar until mixed thoroughly (do not over mix). Pour into baking dish, top with another slice of banana, and place in the air fryer.
3. Bake for 15 minutes, or until slightly browning on the edges (cooking time will depend on your air fryer).
4. Allow to cool completely before serving.

## Air Fryer Banana Pudding

**Prep Time: 10 minutes | Cook Time: 20 minutes | Serves 2**

2 bananas, sliced in half long ways (preferably frozen)
60 ml vanilla extract, divided
60 ml almond extract, divided
250 ml heavy cream (room temperature)
125 ml coconut milk
120 ml water (optional)

1. Preheat your air fryer to 175ºC and spray your pie dish with nonstick spray. In a small saucepan, add the heavy cream, coconut milk and water (if desired) and heat until all the ingredients are just combined together.
2. Add the heavy cream mixture to your sliced banana halves and mix until just combined (do not over mix).
3. Pour the banana mixture into a pie dish and top with half of the vanilla and almond extracts.
4. Bake for 15-20 minutes in your air fryer, or until a toothpick inserted in the center comes out clean.
5. Allow to cool completely before serving.

## Air Fryer Donuts

**Prep Time: 10 minutes | Cook Time: 10 minutes | Serves 8-10**

450 g self-raising flour, sifted
25 g caster sugar (plus extra for dusting)
2 large eggs
50 ml milk (room temperature)
150 g margarine, melted (or butter for greasing the donut hole mould)
30 ml milk (for glaze)

1. In a medium bowl, mix together the flour and sugar until fully combined.
2. In a small bowl, add the eggs and milk and whisk until just combined (do not over mix).
3. Add the egg mixture to your flour mixture and stir with a wisk until just combined (do not over mix).
4. Place your donut hole mould on a baking sheet and pour in your batter until it is half full. Bake at 175ºC for 8-10 minutes and allow to cool on a cooling rack.
5. Repeat the process until you have used all your batter (with one baking sheet).
6. 6. In a small bowl, add melted margarine and milk together and stir until fully combined with no lumps. Pour into an air tight container or baggie and microwave for 30 seconds to melt the margarine.
7. Insert a wooden spoon into the donut hole and dip each side in the glaze, or use a spoon or butter knife to coat.
8. Place glazed donuts on a cooling rack and sprinkle with sugar.
9. Allow to cool completely before serving (I recommend refrigerating for 10-15 minutes before serving).

## Air Fryer Yogurt and Fruit Pie

**Prep Time: 10 minutes | Cook Time: 20 minutes | Serves 2**

175 g icing sugar, sifted
125 ml lemon juice, divided
200 ml yogurt (plain, vanilla, or strawberry), room temperature
165 g fruit (strawberries, blueberries, raspberries), optional

1. In a large bowl whisk together the icing ingredients with 100ml of the lemon juice until smooth.
2. Add the fruit and mix until just combined (do not over mix).
3. Divide into two pie pans. Bake in your air fryer for 15-20 minutes, or until a toothpick inserted in the center comes out clean.
4. Allow to cool completely before serving.

## Air Fryer Apple Fritters

**Prep Time: 10 minutes | Cook Time: 10 minutes | Serves 4**

2 large apples, peeled and chopped into 1" cubes
90 ml water (room temperature)
15 ml lemon juice
0.5 g ground cinnamon, optional
120 g all-purpose flour
1.5 g baking powder
4.5 ml vanilla extract
1 egg (room temperature)

1. In a small bowl, mix together the flour and baking powder.
2. In a medium bowl, add the water, egg, vanilla and lemon juice and whisk until fully combined (do not over mix).
3. Add the flour mixture to your wet ingredients and stir until just combined (do not over mix).
4. Place your apple chunks in the batter and stir to coat evenly. Spray your deep fryer with nonstick spray or lightly grease with vegetable oil.
5. Place your apple fritters in and cook for 5-7 minutes at 175ºC until golden brown.
6. Allow your apples to cool on a cooling rack before serving.

## Air Fryer Beignets

**Prep time: 10 minutes | Cook time: 8 minutes | Serves 4**

1 ml vanilla extract
2 g salt (plus extra for sprinkling)
120 ml warm water (between 105-110 degrees)
120 g all-purpose flour, sifted (plus extra for dusting)
30 ml almond milk (room temperature)

1. Combine all your dry ingredients in a medium bowl. Add the salt, warm water and vanilla; mix with a spatula until just combined (do not over mix).
2. Place your beignet maker on the baking sheet and pour in your batter until it is half full. Bake at 175ºC for 5-8 minutes until golden brown.
3. Repeat the process until you have used all your batter (with one baking sheet).
4. Allow to cool completely before serving (I recommend refrigerating for 10-15 minutes before serving).

## Air Fryer Grilled Peaches

**Prep Time: 10 minutes | Cook Time: 10 minutes | Serves 4**

4 peaches, cut in half and pitted
1.5 ml vanilla extract
60 ml water (room temperature)
30 ml oil

1. In a small bowl, add the water and oil and microwave for 30 seconds until hot (do not over heat). Add in the vanilla extract and stir until fully combined.
2. In a medium bowl, add the peach halves and fully submerge them in your vanilla glaze.
3. Place your peach halves on a baking sheet and spray the top with nonstick spray or lightly grease with vegetable oil. Bake at 175ºC for 10 minutes until golden brown.
4. Allow your peaches to cool on a cooling rack before serving.

Printed in Great Britain
by Amazon

14129069R00040